HIGHER EDUCATION?

HIGHER EDUCATION?

HOW COLLEGES ARE WASTING OUR MONEY AND FAILING OUR KIDS—AND WHAT WE CAN DO ABOUT IT

ANDREW HACKER AND **CLAUDIA DREIFUS**

TIMES BOOKS   HENRY HOLT AND COMPANY   NEW YORK

Times Books
Henry Holt and Company, LLC
Publishers since 1866
175 Fifth Avenue
New York, New York 10010

Henry Holt® is a registered trademark of
Henry Holt and Company, LLC.

Some material in the book has appeared, in slightly different form,
in the *New York Review of Books*.

Library of Congress Cataloging-in-Publication Data
Hacker, Andrew.
  Higher education? : how colleges are wasting our money and failing our kids—and
what we can do about it / Andrew Hacker and Claudia Dreifus.—1st ed.
    p. cm.
  Includes index.
  ISBN 978-0-8050-8734-5
  1. Education, Higher—United States.   2. College costs—United States.   3. College
teachers—United States.   I. Dreifus, Claudia.   II. Title.
  LA227.4.H33 2010+
  378.73—dc22   2010007219

Henry Holt books are available for special promotions and
premiums. For details contact: Director, Special Markets.

First Edition 2010

Designed by Kelly S. Too

Printed in the United States of America
3   5   7   9   11   8   6   4   2

To our country's students, who deserve better

CONTENTS

HIGHER EDUCATION?

INTRODUCTION:
HIGHER EDUCATION?

Every year, in the closing days of summer, a large swath of middle-class Americans engage in a ritual unique to their culture. In driveways from Brookline to Bakersfield, they fill their vehicles with newly purchased goods, ranging from laptops to designer jeans, high-end sneakers, and coffeemakers. In the back sits Jennifer or Jeremy, sending off last-minute text messages to friends. Mom and Dad MapQuest for the best route to towns with names like Chapel Hill, Northfield, and Pomona.

Welcome to the Annual Migration, when some 2.6 million freshmen take their first steps toward adulthood at the nation's 4,352 colleges and universities. For most families, it's an emotional moment. If their destination is one of what *Barron's Guide* calls the "most competitive" institutions—say, Stanford or Emory or Kenyon—the parents feel they've secured a first-class education for their children, plus a reserved place at the table of the nation's elite. If this family is departing for a state-supported institution—perhaps Florida Atlantic or Michigan State—the journey may be another milestone in their quest for upward mobility, a chance for the next generation to move up a rung or two, or even to the top. In either case, this trip will cost far more than the fuel and tolls.

In fact, for those who have to pay the whole tab, a bachelor's degree from a prestigious private college will set a family back more than a quarter of a million dollars. At this writing, a year's tuition, room, and board at the aforementioned Kenyon College comes to $49,290. (True, some families negotiate discounts on the tuition. But at schools like Kenyon a majority of students are or are close to being full payers.) And this doesn't count books, clothes, off-campus snacks, or a summer course at the University of Perugia, which could add another $10,000.

By comparison, the sticker prices at public colleges seem a bargain. Tuitions for in-state residents range from $4,187 at Florida Atlantic to $11,434 at Michigan State. But room and board and other costs are essentially what they are at private schools. Not to mention a car, sorority dues, and football tickets. Thus four years at Boca Raton or East Lansing can easily top $100,000. Moreover, charges at both public and private colleges have more than doubled—in real dollars—compared with a generation ago. Does this signal that the education being provided is twice as good?

This is serious money, by any standard. For most Americans, educating their offspring will be the second-largest outlay they'll ever make. Only the home mortgage will cost more, and you may live forty years in the house. And if parents can't or won't pay, youngsters can find themselves burdened with a staggering load of loans. Graduating with six figures' worth of debts isn't a high-end horror story—it's becoming increasingly common.

So are colleges and universities giving good value for these investments? And what are families buying? Is it training for high-status professions? Or exposure to new ideas, stimulating teachers, and a chance to flex their intellects? Then there's John Dewey's notion of education as preparation for democratic citizenship. And for those attending a sleepaway school, a safe space where the kids can move toward adulthood. Higher education is a

$420 billion industry. What are individuals—and our society as a whole—gaining from it?

The question mark—"?"—in our title is the key to this book, and it will be doing double-duty. As we consider our country's colleges and universities, two questions will recur on every page. The first is how much of what the schools are offering can reasonably be called *education*? For example, we will show that over half of all undergraduates now enroll in vocational *training* programs, which range from standbys like nursing and engineering to new arrivals like resort management and fashion merchandising. While we're sure something is imparted in these classes, we're not comfortable calling it *education*. For us, that designation has to mean more than any instruction coming after the twelfth grade. So enter our second question: even if not vocational, how far can what is being taught and learned reasonably be called *higher*? In our view, college should be a cultural journey, an intellectual expedition, a voyage confronting new ideas and information, together expanding and deepening our understanding of ourselves and the world. Even on academic tracks, we're not persuaded this is happening. For this reason, we'll be taking a close look at fields commonly called the liberal arts. Higher education should set a high bar for itself. It can be done. We've seen it being done.

Moreover, higher education should be open to every young person, and this is an option we can well afford. We confess to being born-again Jeffersonians: we believe everyone has a mind, the capacity to use it, and is entitled to encouragement. Of course, students have to do their share. But the adults who have chosen higher education as their profession have even greater obligations, which we're not convinced they're fulfilling.

Even after acknowledging the difference between education and training, colleges have embraced enterprises that are neither of the two. Universities have become multiversities, staffed by casts of thousands and dedicated to everything from esoteric research to semi-professional athletics. The result has been a significant bloating of the university's original mission and intentions.

In all this, higher education has much in common with the nation's medical system—or, more truthfully, the absence of anything systemic. In both, the costs keep escalating, as a portion of gross domestic product and individual household budgets. (Just as medical bills are the chief cause of bankruptcies, student loans rank high on personal indebtedness.) In neither sphere does it seem possible for anyone to shout *Stop!*—whether it's installing another MRI or when a college decides to shift an athletic team to a more costly division. Fear of too-intrusive government and other over-blown anxieties prevent anyone in authority from saying either leviathan is not delivering on its promises. Perhaps this is just the American way: part-anarchic, part-chaotic, pasted together and responsible to no one. Still, on the educational side, we think there's much that can be improved and we can do a whole lot better.

There is also the mantra that America's medicine and higher education are *the best in the world*. And in some ways, that's accurate. But in both cases this refers to advanced research and specialization, not for a night-shift waitress just diagnosed with cancer or a freshman in the twenty-ninth row in Government 101. In our view, to lead the world has to mean doing your best to make your best accessible to everyone.

Here's our vision for higher education. Our concern, both in this book and for the world at large, is with the undergraduate years. We regard this as a span when young people are sufficiently mature yet still not fully formed, when they can begin to discover themselves and take on the universe. But before we go into particulars, we'd like to specify what we do *not* regard as higher education's obligations.

- As we've noted, we want to distinguish education from *training*. Today's young people are likely to live to be ninety. So there is no need for them to start preparing themselves for careers while they are in their teens. We join Diane Ravitch, who laments that "American higher education has remade itself into a vast job-training program." Indeed, since the mid-1960s, English majors have dropped 51 percent in relation to all degrees, history has experienced a 55 percent decline, and students opting for mathematics are down a whopping 74 percent, despite a putative demand for high-tech experts.

- Nor do we feel undergraduate years should be an apprenticeship for a PhD, let alone a first step toward an academic career. We feel obliged to say this because too many college courses center on topics of interest only to professors. But professors don't have a monopoly on erudition. We believe that the arts and sciences, properly understood, must have a broader and deeper base.

- Perhaps the best way to get support for higher education, or so it is thought, is to warn that the United States is falling behind other nations in skills needed in a competitive world. But the alarms so resoundingly sounded don't decry that we are lagging in philosophy or the humanities. Rather, it's that in countries like China, India, and Korea more students are specializing in the sciences and engineering. The worry is that our workforce—including college graduates—isn't ready for a high-tech age. At this point, we'd only ask, if our economy needs more scientists and engineers, why students aren't enrolling?

- Please give us a hearing while we suggest that a purpose of college is *not* to make students into better citizens. Of course, we'd like everyone to be committed to their communities. But we aren't convinced that we should look to colleges to instill "the knowledge needed to be a reasonably informed citizen in a democracy," as Harvard's Derek Bok puts it. The unstated assumption here is that people who have attended college will end up being *better* citizens than those who have not. For our part, we're not that sure that the kinds of insights and information imparted in college classrooms lead to a higher quality of civic engagement. Nor should we forget highly educated cadres described as "the best and the brightest" have plunged us into unwinnable wars and onto economic shoals. For our own part, we haven't found that ballots cast by college graduates express more cogent thinking than the votes of other citizens. Even now, as a nation, are we more thoughtful than the Illinois farmers who stood for three hours as they pondered the Lincoln-Douglas debates?

• Or listen to Shirley Tilghman, Princeton's president, speaking at its 2009 commencement: "Princeton invests its considerable resources in its students in the belief that we are preparing young men and women to become leaders and change the world for the better." Had we been there, we're sure we would have applauded. Still, to our mind, *leadership* refers to a willingness and ability to rouse people to a party, a purpose, a cause. Here, too, we're not convinced that what happens in classrooms or on campuses nurtures leaders more than other settings—than, for example, back roads of the Mississippi Delta or lettuce fields in California. We will agree that college graduates are more likely to attain *positions* where they rank ahead of others. Yet if Princeton and other colleges boast strong contingents of such people, most of them got to their corner offices by being appointed or promoted. If that's all Shirley Tilghman meant, we can agree.

What do we think *should* happen at college? We want young people to use their minds as they never have before, thinking hard about realities and issues that strain their mental powers. They should be urged to be imaginative and inquiring, to take risks without having to worry about their transcripts or alienating their teachers. To quote a friend, colleges should be making their undergraduates more *interesting* people. Higher education is an ongoing conversation, created for students poised at adulthood, which can and will continue throughout their lives.

This is a natural process, one for which young people are already fitted. After all, curiosity comes with being human. The problem today is that too much college teaching seeks to channel thinking into tight academic grooves. That is why we've deliberately avoided using terms like *cognitive* and *analytic*, or phrases like *critical thinking* and *moral reasoning*. There's nothing inherently wrong with these rubrics, it's just that they've been recast to force freshmen to view the world through professorial prisms.

In fact, there are thousands of undergraduate teachers who regard education as a lively interchange. We have sat, admiringly, in many of their classes. Yet few of them are recognized beyond their campuses, since they haven't conducted the research their disciplinary peers demand. So we'll cite some better-known models. There is Princeton's Paul Krugman, a Nobel Laureate, who makes economics explicable in the *New York Times*. Or Jill Lepore of Harvard, who brings history to life for readers of *The New Yorker*. Cosmologist Lawrence Krauss of Arizona State University, who loves meeting with high school students and brings his Nobelist friends to chat with them. These professors do not set boundaries between how they address a general audience and what they do in their classrooms. For them—and for us—it's all higher education.

Since we acknowledge that higher education is so massive and sprawling, we had to decide how much we could responsibly cover in a single book. This is what we decided.

- Our focus would be on undergraduates seeking bachelor's degrees. Even allowing for high attrition, which we'll be discussing, these candidates are the largest constellation in the higher education universe. So when we refer to community colleges, it will be to focus on how well they usher their students into four-year schools.

- We decided, after some soul searching, not to separate out the country's fifty-two women's colleges and eighty-five historically black institutions. Or, for that matter, sectarian schools like Yeshiva University in New York, Brigham Young in Utah, or Regent University in Virginia. Plus a host of good colleges under religious auspices, like Augustana in South Dakota and Saint Anselm in New Hampshire. Or our military academies. We respect them all and the roles they play. We simply felt we couldn't do justice to so wide a swath.

- For-profit colleges—notably Kaplan, Phoenix, and DeVry—are fast-growing newcomers to higher education. In just five years, 2003 to 2008, their numbers grew from 300 to close to 500. Because their students come and go, it's not easy to obtain reliable headcounts, and most are not pursuing degrees. Still, in the years cited, their bachelor's graduates more than doubled, from 31,155 to 70,765, the latter figure comprising 4.6 percent of all such awards. It remains to be seen how employers, graduate schools, and professional licensing bodies will view these degrees. We'll be watching.

This said, we do have a chapter where we will focus on *distance learning,* where most or all of the work can be done at home or otherwise away from a campus classroom. So we will be reporting on what happens when laptop screens replace a sentient teacher, plus how student participation is affected and performance is assessed. We've tallied what is gained and what is lost. It's our hope that this book and the issues we discuss will encourage debate about this vital sector of our national life.

Our principal premise is that higher education has lost track of its original and enduring purpose: to challenge the minds and imaginations of this nation's young people, to expand their understanding of the world, and thus of themselves. At all too many of our colleges this mission no longer has priority. We will show how our campuses have become preserves for adult careers; how professors, administrators, and, yes, presidents, have used ostensible centers of learning to pursue their own interests and enjoyments.

We believe these turnings can and should be changed. In our view, the first step is to take an unsparing look at what has been happening in the name of an honored calling. That is just what we will do in the chapters that follow.

PART 1

WHAT WENT WRONG?

· 1 ·

THE WORLD OF THE PROFESSORIATE

A few years back, the political science department of Queens College, part of the City University of New York, put out a call for an assistant professor to teach basic classes in American government. In a tight job market, this was an unusually good opportunity. The position was "tenure track," which meant that in six years' time it could lead to a lifetime appointment. The pay was above average. Moreover, this was a rare opening in geographically desirable New York City. Most beginning professors are forced to start out in towns like Ames, Iowa, or San Marcos, Texas.

As it happened, a young political scientist just finishing his dissertation at a top research university made it to the short list. His research—"An Algorithm for Statutory Reconciliation in Bicameral Legislatures"—had a trendy feel to it. His mentors had sent glowing recommendations, casting him as a rising academic star.

Yet, on campus at Queens College, Golden Boy's presentation, meant to showcase his intellectual breadth and teaching style, failed to impress. At an interview with the departmental chair, he made no inquiries about the school or its students. Nor did he ask the one question that every career coach claims is essential in a job interview: "What can I do for *you*?"

Instead, his first question was: "What's the teaching load here?" "Three and three," the chair answered politely, meaning that her staff taught three courses each semester.

"That won't work," he quickly returned. "I have my research to continue with and, as you heard, it's important. Where I did my doctorate, it was two and two. By the way, how do your sabbaticals work?" He was told one came every seventh year, after six of teaching.

The candidate winced. "I couldn't consider that. At other schools, it's a year off after three. If I were to come here, we'd have to make some special arrangement."

This young man never got a callback, which we suspect must have puzzled him. True, this episode occurred several years ago, when young stars felt they could write their own tickets. Today, hiring freezes are the rule, and there can be several hundred applicants for any open position. Current candidates accept the templates of the job, no questions asked. So here's our reason for recalling this interview. Despite the downturn in the economy, the academic culture that produced this young man hasn't changed. He was only emulating the ways of his mentors—in this case, to negotiate for as little teaching as possible, with ample time for research and the support it would need. In the entitled world where he'd been nurtured, a place so different from the rest of society, there was nothing odd about going to an interview and, in effect, asking, "How little do I have to do?" Moreover, if he happens to get one of the now-scarce openings, and in time achieves the protection of tenure, we doubt if we'll see him volunteering to teach Political Science 101.

Ah, the professoriate! It's an alternate universe. While the rest of working Americans endure foremen and supervisors, professors often get to select their colleagues, vote on raises and promotions, and even in some instances vote out their bosses. The schools almost function for them, for their aspirations and interests. Students come and go every four years, administrators will move on, but the tenured stay on in Bloomington, College Park, and Chapel Hill, accumulating power, controlling resources, reshaping the university according to their needs. Lost on the Professorial Campus is the primacy of students and, for reasons that sometimes seem mystifying, an appreciation of an activity as joyful and useful as teaching.

Think of the American colleges and universities as bound by a caste system, with different status grades assigned to the approximately 860,000 men and women the Department of Labor counts as full-time faculty. (Part-timers come and go, often teaching a single course, sometimes on several campuses, so it's impossible to pinpoint their exact numbers.)

The top caste consists of some 320,000 associate and full professors, most of whom have tenure or will soon receive that award. The candidate we mentioned was already envisioning himself at that rank, which partly explains his entitled demeanor. Below them, there are about 170,000 assistant professors, most of them on the "tenure track" that we alluded to earlier. Usually, those already on that track ultimately receive that promotion since they were carefully vetted and the people who hired them don't want it felt that the department made a mistake.

Most of the other full-time faculty, the third tier in the caste system, are instructors and lecturers who aren't in line for promotion and who handle introductory sections at modest salaries and some benefits. (A number are faculty spouses unable to find other employment.) This tier also contains visiting instructors, who usually come for a year to replace professors on sabbaticals. The fourth and fifth castes are made up of part-time adjuncts and graduate assistants. They are the contingent people of the campus—exploitable, disposable, impoverished by low wages. They do the bulk of the undergraduate teaching at many universities.

So this chapter will focus on upward of half a million men and women holding the three professor ranks (assistant, associate, and full) and who make up about 57 percent of full-time faculty personnel. This professorial class controls what happens on many a campus and, too often, self-interested management is the result.

In theory, education is supposed to be a public service: like health care, firefighting, national parks. And by and large that describes the motivations of teachers from kindergarten through high school. But as we ascend to colleges and universities—the preserve of professors—self-interest, strengthened by a narrow sense of self-definition, begins to set in.

It starts with how professors identify with their disciplines. Imagine that we were to say that the employees in an enterprise all brought a central part of their personal history with them to work, and insisted that it govern how they did their jobs. Thus Methodists would contend that they had to adhere to their liturgy, with Baptists and Catholics and Jews making similar claims. All would argue that their creeds are crucial to their identities. Nor is it just how they've been raised; it is who they *are*.

As the social psychologist Gerd Gigerenzer, formerly of the University of Chicago and now the director of one of the branches of Berlin's Max Planck Institute, told us, "I believe it's one of the worst things that's happened, that people identify with a discipline or a sub-discipline in a way like members of a political movement identify with their party."

But this is exactly how college faculties operate. Under the venerable headings we see in college catalogs: physics, history, mathematics, drama, sociology, literature. The rigidity of these disciplines atomizes campuses, transforming departments into fiefdoms and actually hindering the transmission of knowledge. PhD programs, where fledgling professors are trained, are much like seminaries: elders impart the lore and litany of a liturgy.

Were anything like this to occur at the Boeing company, few Dreamliners would ever get aloft.

During those postgraduate years, a candidate in anthropology *becomes an anthropologist*. So the discipline that a candidate chooses—its mores, its mentality, its methods—comes to express not only their profession but also an academic's identity. They begin to see and understand the world through the lens of anthropology. "Whenever I watch people interacting in a stadium, a subway, a supermarket checkout," a young scholar told us, "I find myself seeing tribal rites or kinship networks."

Despite much lip service to interdisciplinary studies, on most campuses anthropologists have only passing contact with their colleagues in sociology, although an outsider might think they have much to share. Even sociology and social psychology have different vocabularies, methods, and explanatory models. Once upon a time, Harvard established a Department of Social Relations, in hope of integrating teaching and research in supposedly kindred fields. The joint department had a short life span. The professors were ill at ease outside their home territories. Probably the only area where interdisciplinary work has had any palpable impact is in the hard sciences, where physics, chemistry, biology, and computation have combined to uncover new knowledge about our macro and micro universes. A job shortage in the world of physics has made interdisciplinary studies, particularly in biology, attractive to young physicists—science has a growing number of people who now dub themselves "biophysicists."

But in the social sciences and the humanities, doubtless because those disciplines are less secure about what they actually do, the borders remain rigidly guarded. Scott Page, who holds a joint position in economics and political science at the University of Michigan, told us that his colleagues "spend years keeping up with one discipline and want to continue on that path; it's like a zoo where each species is in a separate cage." Once, he took a biologist whose paper he'd found "amazing" to lunch and she told him that this was the first time in all her years on campus that she'd heard from someone in a different field.

At a reinvented Arizona State University, Michael Crow, its president, has tried to break down some of the disciplinary walls. He has abolished whole departments, using senior appointments skillfully and creating new interdisciplinary institutes. His professoriate, or at least some parts of it, has been outraged. This suggests to us he is doing something right.

Professors are often isolated not only from those outside their disciplines but also from the outside world. In the nineteenth century, when most colleges and universities were founded, the idea took hold that they should be situated far away from the sordid cities. It's a tradition that holds till this day. Hence Colby College is in Waterville, Maine (15,606), Western Oregon in Monmouth (7,741), Kenyon College in Gambier, Ohio (1,817). Even state universities are sequestered in towns like Eugene, Norman, and Tuscaloosa. We'll leave it to others to judge the extent that a verdant campus keeps corruption at bay.

What interests us now is the effect this isolation has on members of the faculties. The first fact is that given the reclusive setting, the college is the only game in town. For all intents and purposes, nothing else is going on. So whatever happens on the campus becomes the focus of attention, looming larger than it is or needs to be. A friend who taught for many years at Cornell told us about faculty parties, where one might expect cerebral conversations on the state of the universe.

"It didn't work that way," she confessed. "We had been thrown together so much that we all knew what everyone thought." So after a Julia Child dinner, talk would turn to a new associate provost, vandalism at a fraternity party, or plans for a multilevel garage. "You find yourself having strong opinions on even the smallest matters," our informant added. "In fact, every incident becomes an issue." Since moving to an urban university, where she and her colleagues also have other lives, it's easier for her to see just how insular her world in the more removed setting had become.

Factionalized politics and isolation also become a way for professors to maintain their privileged environments. But it is not the only way. Maybe most important, professors in many departments have been able to take workplace democracy to an unprecedented level. Through self-governance, the interests of one class of employees, the tenured professors, predominate.

Self-governance, perhaps unsurprisingly, uses a great deal of teachers' time and energy. As we traveled to college campuses, the plaints we heard from professors most frequently centered on the time spent serving on committees. Such meetings are usually put under the heading of *service*, a third requisite for promotion and recognition along with teaching and research. But it can come close to consuming as much time. And that's the problem.

Certainly, people in other occupations meet occasionally to share ideas and agree on decisions. When Claudia's colleagues at the *New York Times* meet on Tuesday afternoons, they keep each other abreast of projects and share sources and information about new developments on their beats. It's a wonderful seminar in contemporary science. Sometimes committees will be formed to solve specific tasks, but they terminate when the project is completed.

Not so in the academic world. Not only are most college committees permanent; new ones are formed every semester. Carleton College in Northfield, Minnesota (population 17,147) has a fine liberal arts program, engaged students, and a dedicated faculty. Despite these and other virtues, it is severely afflicted with the committee virus. According to its website, it has *sixty-eight* of them, which we calculate comes to one such entity for every three members of its faculty. (And this doesn't count committees within departments or divisions.) Here are several that caught our attention:

Accessibility Awareness Committee

Faculty Compensation Committee

Language Requirement Exemption Committee

Animal Care and Use Committee

Recreation Center Advisory Committee

Junior Faculty Affairs Committee

Sexual Harassment & Sexual Assault Committee

Committee on Convocation & Common Conversation

We have no doubt that justifications can be adduced for each of these, as well as the roughly sixty committees we haven't listed. Yet staffing all these committees will keep many a professor occupied with tasks that have little to do with the actual teaching of their students.

When we inquired of our professional colleagues whether faculty, students—everyone—would benefit from a little less consultation, we were asked if we preferred that the adjudication of sexual assaults be left to appointed administrators. Or if we'd wanted the concerns of junior faculty to be handled solely by the provost rather than a panel of colleagues and peers. Or whether having a recreation committee isn't a better way to schedule swimming hours than by using a desk-bound director.

There is a general consensus within the professoriate that administrators are a kind of class enemy and a danger, rather than facilitators of a joint enterprise. In the end, we are being asked to accept that committees like Carleton's are patently needed, since the democratic ethos is predicated on participation and consultation. But we can't help but wonder: can there be too much public input? And we can't help but remember that there are huge sectors of every university's community—contingent faculty we'll write about later—that have less than no voice in governance.

Committees are not only busywork, they are a surrogate for faculty members who have long since given up on scholarship. Rebecca Chopp noticed this when she first arrived at Colgate to assume the presidency. "The same core people would come to all faculty meetings," she told us. "But they weren't our researchers and/or our great teachers." A Cornell professor reported something similar: "Many of my colleagues haven't written a word in their field for the past twenty years. But they handily turn out forty-page committee reports."

Committees also proliferate because academics, to an unusual degree, want to feel they are being consulted, not just on major policies but about everything else that happens on their campus. Rebecca Chopp told us that her faculty at Colgate wanted to establish a "strategic planning committee" to oversee all presidential decisions. "I told them, 'Try it if you like; you're going to be working twenty-four hours a day to keep up with me.' The proposal was dropped, but it testifies to an enormous anxiety that they've lost control of the institution."

When faculty members do have power, they often use it to resist. When Chopp tried to enlist faculty to invite students into their homes so they could see professors in another setting, she found few takers. "They have tenure," she said, and sighed. "They do whatever they want."

Some brave spirits defy the participatory tide. When Debora Spar, who'd been a dean at Harvard Business School, started as president of Barnard College she sought to cut down on staff duplication. Instead of assembling yet another committee, she turned to the McKinsey firm, which sent two seasoned consultants, both women and one a Barnard graduate, to investigate and then present recommendations. Perhaps it wasn't participatory democracy. But in a recessionary time, stern measures were needed if the college wanted to preserve what was really important. We suspect Spar knew that a faculty committee simply wouldn't have the stomach to dismiss colleagues with whom they regularly had lunch.

Moves like Spar's to reduce governance by committee, however, are rare. At many colleges, professors like to feel they have co-equal status with their president; at some schools, Harvard notably, they have. Laurence Summers, the only Harvard president forced to leave office after a no-confidence vote, did so not because of his notorious statements about scientific women but because many regarded him as aggrandizing too much power. At most schools, the professoriate want to believe they are partners in "shared governance" with the president; Summers, they felt, didn't share.

There certainly are schools where faculty votes sometimes put the brakes on administrative abuses and where professors can be useful whistleblowers. But the committees are also roadblocks to genuine leadership. We remember a story told to us by the late Clinton Rossiter of Cornell. He and a group of professors had been invited to meet with the president, who proposed creating a college-wide "great issues" course. It would be taken by all seniors in their final term, aiming at summing up ideas basic to a liberal education. "The president's presentation had barely begun," Rossiter recalled, "when my colleagues pronounced it an abominable idea. They told the president he had no business thinking about the curriculum, and they would in no way assist with the project. It expired that morning."

Then there's the pay. Professors are fond of saying they didn't choose their profession for the money. And it's true that apart from coveted coaches and medical school stars, salaries top off at six figures. Still, it's not self-evident that many academics would be doing better in more demanding occupations. According to the American Association of University Professors, the average pay for full professors, a rank usually reached by one's early forties, came to $108,749 in 2008–9. By comparison, salaried lawyers averaged $91,052; for chemical engineers the figure was $80,392, and financial analysts came in at $71,656.

All in all, the academy isn't poverty row, as averages for full professors show. Thus there are generous salaries at Northwestern ($161,800) and Emory ($153,400). But second-tier public institutions like the University of Delaware ($130,000) and Michigan State ($121,900) aren't very far behind. What we found interesting was that many independent colleges are also in this league. Full professors at Bates now average $113,400, at Occidental they get $111,100, and at Grinnell it's $113,100. Even less-known schools like Elon in North Carolina ($102,400) and Wheaton in Massachusetts ($104,300) cross the six-figure threshold.

What we feel obliged to add is that at smaller colleges, few professors ever leave. In large part, that's because these professors lack reputations that might make them sought by other schools. In sheer market terms, they're overpaid, since they have nowhere else to go. And stars seldom leave simply for the money. Recently, Claudia was at a dinner with an A-list scientist. He had just moved to Columbia from the California public system. "My former chancellor tells people I moved because of the budget cuts—it's his argument against them," he said. "But that wasn't it at all! I left because I wanted to be in New York."

While not up with Wall Street, academic salaries have been rising faster than the cost of living, and are well ahead of the earnings of average working men and women. Since 1985, measured in constant-value dollars, salaries of Harvard's full professors have risen by 53 percent. Stanford's real increase has been 57 percent, and at Princeton, it's been 64 percent. In the public sector, the pay is lower, but there too professors' checks are well ahead of inflation. Texas's full professors are now 46 percent better off compared with 1985, and at North Carolina, the gain has been 56 percent. Professors may talk as if they're alienated and unappreciated. However, their take-home pay doesn't substantiate those feelings.

So what's fair pay? It's an old conundrum. Why does a brain surgeon make ten times as much as a firefighter? After all, both are skilled and save lives. We won't rehearse the reasons people give to justify their incomes, because they are almost always self-serving, especially in the higher brackets. What we will do, though, is lay out the basic academic workload. That is, the number of hours when professors have to be at stated places at specified times. Those places are their classrooms, along with their offices where they post hours to see students.

We've chosen two colleges and have calculated the working schedules of their full professors. The first is Kenyon, an excellent liberal arts college in Ohio, where the teaching load is five courses each two-semester year; in academic parlance, *three and two*. We also assume these professors hold two office hours per week, during each fifteen-week semester. But there's another element in the equation. Every seventh year, Kenyon faculty members receive a fully paid semester off from teaching. So factoring in sabbaticals, Kenyon professors average 381 classroom and office hours per year. (The salaried lawyers we alluded to typically average 1,960 courtroom and office hours annually.)

Our second choice was Yale. There, professors in departments like economics and psychology teach *two and one*. So in one semester they have only one class, and thus don't need as many office hours. Yale also gives them what it calls a "triennial leave of absence." After five semesters of teaching, they have a fully paid semester off. So the workload of Yale's professors works out to 213 annual hours in a classroom or their office. To extend the exercise, we now include the facts that full professors at Kenyon average $92,100, while at Yale it's $174,700.

Given these salaries, Kenyon's professors are being paid $242 per hour, while Yale's hourly rate is $820.

We can already hear anguished cries from the faculty club. Professors will predictably insist that there's far more to their jobs than the hours we've cited. Academics routinely say they put in at least sixty hours a week.

We readily acknowledge they do *something* outside their classroom and office hours. But the great bulk of it is less real than contrived: committees, department meetings, faculty senates, and yes, what they call their research, the utility of which we question in a later chapter.

Well, then, how about preparing classes, reading examinations and papers, and directing honors theses? We'll grant that we haven't counted these tasks in our basic hours. Here's why. The basic hours are simply when we can say with some certainty that this is where a professor will be. But we have no way of knowing how much time many of them really devote to revising lectures, restructuring courses, or organizing new ones. So we want to place the burden on those who claim they work at updating their courses, to make a convincing case that all that redrafting is essential. And of course there are professors who never change their notes. (Or, in techo-teaching, their PowerPoint slides.)

A story is told of a classroom where all the students were busily scribbling as the professor droned on. All, that is, but one, a young woman in the back row, who wrote down nary a word. How so? She had with her the notes that her mother had taken for that class during her own student days.

Of course, there are professors who read examinations carefully and fill the margins with helpful comments, which we're sure is much the case at Kenyon. When that's so, we'll be pleased to stipulate that they are putting in more than the basic hours. But at Yale, we're less sure, since a great deal of the reading and grading is done by graduate assistants.

The best-endowed campuses don't stop with munificent salaries. (We deem $820 an hour to be a generous wage.) It may make sense to allow Stanford faculty children to go there for free, but it should be added that this $37,380 annual benefit is entirely tax-free. And also tax-free is Stanford's picking up half the tab if its professors' progeny go away to Harvard or Haverford. At the same time that the scholars at Stanford's Hoover Institution rail against welfare programs, their university maintains some 700 rent-subsidized faculty apartments. It gets even better for those preferring to purchase. Newly tenured associate professors can, for nine years, draw an added $21,500 annually toward a mortgage. And it will lend full professors half the mortgage on properties costing up to $1.2 million, at below-market rates. This fringe benefit, Stanford says on its website, enables faculty "to purchase a more costly home than if he/she used only a conventional mortgage." Princeton has a similar program for its senior faculty, although it comes with a caveat. Any home to be subsidized must be within eight miles of the university. We suspect there are some interesting stories behind that restriction.

We've shown how little is asked from professors during the months when classes are taught. But the academic profession is the only one we know of that gives its employees prolonged respites from work while their paychecks keep coming. We're talking, of course, about sabbaticals. Until recently, the term was construed literally: the Sabbath being the seventh day, so sabbaticals were to come every seventh year. More exactly, six years of work would be followed by either a full year off at half-pay or a half-year at full pay. But that's changed at many schools. Even at the City University of New York, not the most solvent institution, professors who take a full year off now receive 80 percent of their salary.

There were once alternating views on what professors were supposed to do when they were freed from teaching. The first was that sabbaticals would give them time to revise their courses, catch up on reading, perhaps spend the year abroad. The reasoning was that though teaching can be invigorating, its daily chores didn't allow for uninterrupted reflection. So unlike accountants and engineers, it was said, professors must have additional time to recharge their intellects.

But even liberal arts schools and lower-tier state colleges now expect that research will appear in a published format. After all, faculty publications are what give a campus status. Whether the push for research has gone too far is a question we'll deal with in detail later on. Here we'll merely note that a friend of ours, the president of a liberal arts college in the Northeast, was nonplussed when she saw a tenured "yoga professor" on the sabbatical list. The experience made her think about pruning the physical education requirements and outsourcing yoga-minded students to a studio in the town.

At Yale, as we've seen, the faculty members no longer need to wait seven years, but can now spend every third year away. At Harvard, even untenured assistant professors get a fully paid year to complete a promotion-worthy book. Thus in a recent year, of its history department's six assistant professors, only two were on hand to teach classes. In Harvard's department of philosophy that same year, almost half of its full-time faculty—eight of its seventeen professors—were away on sabbaticals. Of course, it was the students who paid. Many of their undergraduate courses were canceled or given by one-year visitors unfamiliar with the byways of the university.

We grant that Harvard is especially well endowed—or at least it was until the meltdown of 2008. But it sets a standard other colleges hope to emulate, which then affects how they will parcel out whatever funds they have. Even at Williams, which originally put teaching first, a third of the faculty is absent in a typical year. Nor are parents told how much of what they remit for tuition goes toward paying professors not to teach.

We now want to raise a seemingly naïve question. Why should students pay for time when they won't be seeing their professors, especially when the chief motive for publishing is to enhance personal careers? In other occupations, when people feel there is something they want to write, they do it on their own time and at their own expense. So it has occurred to us that if sabbaticals were curtailed or even ended, the quality of academic publications might actually improve because what was produced would have been done by professors burning to put words on paper, or at least on an Internet site.

Though often exceptionally well paid and able to exercise more control over their lives than the members of practically any other profession, college and university professors often express surprisingly low levels of job satisfaction. To paraphrase W. S. Gilbert, a professor's lot is not a happy one. In our travels, we've attended quite a few academic social functions. Whether we were in Berkeley or Boston, the talk was similar: the students are semi-literate; the school's president is anti-intellectual; the new parking rules are inequitable; and there's this boorish colleague who filibusters at meetings.

At the end of the day, this strange little world often alienates the genuinely smart and idealistic. Many of the best people find it intolerable, clearing the path for careerists. Claudia recently heard from Holly Stocking, a friend who'd taken early retirement from teaching journalism at Indiana University. "I remember my first year in the harness, thinking, 'Now I have to construct myself as an expert,'" she told us. "But it always felt a little Machiavellian. Creating new bits of knowledge was paramount, while applying old knowledge and cultivating wisdom were given short shrift. Eventually, the healthy part of myself said, 'Enough!'"

· 2 ·

ADMINISTRATIVE OVERLOAD

Williams College, situated in a rural corner of Massachusetts, is the second-oldest college in the state. Its bucolic campus hosts just under two thousand students, attracted by its small size and traditional liberal arts curriculum. Williams is precisely the kind of place that one expects a generous faculty-to-student ratio. Attentive, caring teachers are usually what one has in mind when selecting a small undergraduate college. What may be more surprising to parents wondering if they should write the hefty checks that Williams asks for is not its faculty ratio, but the proportion of *administrators* to students.

Williams's own reports to the U.S. Department of Education reveal that 695 of its 984 employees, or over 70 percent, are doing something other than teaching. Among them are 84 athletic coaches; 73 fund-raisers; a 42-member information-technology crew; a 29-person staff at its art museum, as well as 120 people in buildings and on grounds; and 124 in dining services, the latter including 26 dishwashers. The school has a "babysitting coordinator," a "spouse/partner employment counselor," and a "queer life coordinator" (their designation).

Are all these people and positions necessary?

Mind you, we don't mean to pick on Williams. The growth of administration there merely mirrors a national trend. Between 1976 and 2007, the ratio of college administrators to students basically doubled. In 1976, for every 1,000 students, there were 32 adults holding non-faculty positions. By 2007, the most recent available year, there were 63 such people for every 1,000 students. Nor are we talking about groundskeepers or cafeteria workers, although we will later. Right now our interest is in professionals like admissions officers and assistant deans. Since 1976, their campus presence has more than tripled. True, the number of students has also grown, but by less than the rate of the administrative phalanx.

For a look at these positions, we examined employment openings advertised in the *Chronicle of Higher Education* (rate: $2,936 per quarter-page). Most of the positions are of relatively recent vintage. In the past, colleges were seeking a new provost or a registrar. Here are just a few that caught our eye:

Sustainability Director

Residential Communications Coordinator

Coordinator of Learning Immersion Experiences

Senior Specialist of Assessment

Director of Knowledge Access Services

Dietetic Internship Director

Credential Specialist

Director of Active and Collaborative Engagement

Director for Learning Communities and First Year Success

Vice President of Student Success

Bureaucrats in every endeavor seek to enlarge their responsibilities; the more of them there are, the more indispensable they seem. In particular, they become adept at weaving webs of words, sentences, and paragraphs to justify their presence. So in scanning the positions we've just listed, we can be sure that for each of them, there will be someone ready to explain that it serves a vital purpose.

Vice President for Student Success? We all want to raise graduation rates, so more professional interventions are needed to reach that goal.

Residential Communications Coordinator? Dormitory living can be isolating, even threatening, possibly leading to suicidal thoughts. So adult staffing should be available.

Credential Specialist? Since higher education relies on folders filled with diplomas, certificates, and transcripts, colleges should have experts to ensure their authenticity.

Dietetic Internship Director? Given a national concern with obesity and nutrition, guiding students into these careers is hardly frivolous.

Each of these offices and programs, and the people in them, began with a plausible rationale and a credible purpose. The Williams babysitting service helps both faculty parents and students who want to make some extra money. And since it isn't easy being gay or lesbian while away at college, a queer life coordinator can help them focus on their studies. But though it's one thing to say a service is useful, that doesn't prove it's necessary. Or, for that matter, that it enhances the college's educational mission, even indirectly. Or that one needs an administrator, often with staff and supportive personnel for these services.

A way to start is by comparing a pair of schools. Much is made of student-to-faculty ratios, which are often used as indices of the attention undergraduates get. So we will add our own student-administration parallel.

Swarthmore is one of the nation's most affluent colleges. Prior to the 2008 economic meltdown, its endowment was generating $163,074 per year for each of its 1,472 students. One of the ways this money was spent was to hire 253 administrators, presumably to enhance the quality of its students' college experience. At most recent count, Swarthmore retained 170 such adults for each 1,000 of its undergraduates.

Along with Swarthmore, Wilmington College is also a Quaker school, having 1,490 students on its Ohio campus. But there the resemblance ends. Wilmington's endowment yields $2,275 per student, which is nickels and dimes when compared with Swarthmore's dividends. One consequence is that it has only 81 non-instructional people on the payroll, which yields a ratio of 54 administrators per 1,000 students. Yet from everything we've heard, Wilmington is serving its undergraduates very adequately, even with less than a third as many functionaries as its wealthier sister school. We often hear that countries with fewer doctors turn out to be healthier than their more heavily medicated counterparts. We're beginning to think that this finding might also apply to higher education.

Administrators don't simply absorb salaries. They also need physical space. These facilities are often underwritten by bond issues, which oblige colleges to make annual interest payments, not to mention redeeming the principal at the end. Lourdes College has recently opened a student-outreach center, and American University now has a career-center suite. Troy University provides counseling laboratories and Agnes Scott College has a multi-faith meditation room. When Kenyon College erected its Taj Mahal of an athletics center, it also housed these administrative officers: Sports Information Director, Sports Facilities Director, Assistant

Athletics Director of Compliance (who doubles as the Director of Aquatics), Coordinator for Lifetime Fitness, Intramural and Club Sport Coordinator, Equipment Manager, someone to do "data entry," and more than forty coaches for what is now the expected spectrum of sports, including softball, field hockey, football, swimming and diving, lacrosse, golf, tennis, and track and field. Also, its sushi bar requires chefs, and the coffee station needs baristas. Meanwhile, Kenyon's philosophy department has to get along with five faculty members. Given this imbalance, we couldn't help but wonder, is this a college or a resort? We certainly know which part is growing fastest.

Administrators have also proliferated as colleges take on more "caretaking" functions for increasingly protected students. Parents of Williams students are informed that "you can surprise your son or daughter with a 'Special Occasion Cake' from dining services." And if the youngster overdoses on the pastry, the college also has services for those "students who need assistance with diet or health problems, or who are interested in learning more about nutrition and its relationship to wellness."

It's not easy to argue that any of this makes an educational contribution. Rather, the schools respond to an amenities arms race, aimed at seventeen-year-olds who are thought to base their college decision more on hot tubs than classes. When we anonymously joined a Dartmouth tour for potential applicants and their parents, the most typical questions were about parking spaces and fraternity dues. But it's up to the colleges to stress their educational purpose. How about treating applicants to a special lecture by an exciting professor? Dartmouth visitors might take away a lot more from a half hour with brilliant theologian Susannah Heschel than a trip to its hockey rink.

If colleges are proliferating services for students, they're also devising new bureaus to support the faculty. Duke employs a quasi-agent/editor who helps professors shape their book proposals and find publishers. Dartmouth, the scene of a decades-long war between conservative graduates and its more liberal college administration, has a staff tasked with mollifying the alumni. Big universities have special writers to help faculty peg grant proposals to whatever new disciplines are currently in vogue, like homeland security or green technology. In the search for federal dollars, some larger schools employ their own lobbyists, just as public universities have staffs to interface with their state legislatures. Some hire risk management specialists to anticipate lawsuits, alongside their lawyers who handle those that get filed.

And every school from Megalopolis U to St. Trinian's Junior College has communications officers, more prosaically known as publicists. Our colleges and universities are about as subtle in their quest for attention as Paris Hilton. Thus Claudia and her colleagues at the *New York Times* find their inboxes laden with press releases suggesting "stories" like these:

- A pair of social psychologists at Oklahoma State University have published a paper showing that "single women prefer to date attached men."

- The University of Pittsburgh communications office has experts available to "comment on the 150th anniversary of the oil industry and its birth in Western Pennsylvania."

- A professor at New York University's Polytechnic engineering school has discovered a relationship between the tempo of popular music and the state of the stock market.

Nor is all administrative growth internally fueled. Research universities are required to hire extra staff to cope with the plethora of regulations that come with governmental funding for research. Every school, for example, that accepts research dollars is required to set up an Institutional Review Board (IRB) to monitor what is called "human experimentation." That, too, adds to the administrative overload, and worse.

IRBs began in the 1970s in order to prevent experiments by medical schools that resulted in physical harm or death. Today they cover almost every type of academic inquiry, including in the social sciences, humanities, even journalism. The boards, most ominously, have become a quiet but potent threat to academic freedom.

At the University of Missouri, a graduate student in journalism named Michael Carney, as part of his master's program, planned to ask reporters and editors in the state capitol about their use of polling in election coverage. Carney's university IRB ordered him to halt work on his project because he'd failed to warn his sources—practicing journalists—that they might suffer distress as a result of the interview process. Mr. Carney, a reporter to his soul, went ahead with his project anyway. He was backed by his journalism school advisors.

How did this happen? How did universities come to be such behemoths, providing plush and numerous jobs for administrators, often at the expense of their own students? It all started with an unlikely revolutionary named Clark Kerr, who headed the University of California from 1958 to 1967, which turned into an explosive decade. On first encounter, you might have mistaken him for your accountant: high forehead, rimless glasses, an unmemorable voice. But Clark Kerr was a man with a mission. In his view, the very word *university* was a relic of a fast-receding past. Its unitary prefix suggested a single focus, which was teaching, mainly of undergraduates, requiring little more than classrooms, a library, and some modest laboratories. All that had to change, Kerr asserted, and California would show the way. So he coined a new idiom, *multiversity*: an institution willing to take on any assignments related to knowledge, no matter how remote the association. Heading the list would of course be research, with sponsors including corporations and the military, even clandestine agencies. In a series of 1963 lectures, he informed the larger society that the nation's campuses were ready to be of service.

For Kerr's vision to be achieved, his multiversities first had to build up their base. And this, ironically, was made possible by new influxes of undergraduates, whose arrival moved higher education to center stage. In many ways, the decades following World War II were unique. Still, higher education has a long history. In particular, it's been a saga of increasing access, with each year advancing toward a day when most Americans will have a degree.

In the midst of the Civil War, in 1862, Congress took time off to pass the Morrill Act, which mandated that every state support a public university. Whereas the bill specified attention to "agriculture and the mechanic arts," its overall aim was to extend *both* "liberal and practical education" to new segments of the population. The roster resulting from the bill now includes over one hundred schools, ranging from Iowa State and Michigan State to Rutgers and MIT as well as Florida A&M and Alcorn State. Though all still have schools of agriculture and engineering, they also have liberal arts divisions, with serious programs in fields like literature and philosophy.

Still, by 1940, as the Depression was ending, less than 10 percent of young Americans were receiving degrees. That would change with the passage of the GI Bill in 1944, which told every man and woman who had served in World War II that he or she could attend college at public expense. Almost half who had been in uniform—7.8 million of 16 million—accepted that offer. As expected and intended, they raised overall enrollments, but the influx didn't stop with veterans. Indeed, their decisions kindled a desire for college in social classes that had never contemplated that option. By 1950, after most of the veterans had graduated, 18 percent of the college-age cohort were getting degrees, over twice the number at the start of the decade.

Other forces were less legislative than demographic. With the close of World War II, people began making up for babies they didn't have during the Depression and while men were overseas. From 1946 through 1964, couples of all classes were having three or four children, more than anyone had anticipated. By the 1960s, the first of this baby boom cohort were old enough for college, and many were ready to go. Between 1960 and 1970, undergraduate enrollments doubled once again, another unprecedented increase, with most of these students being the first in their families to go to college.

Among the converging trends, the economy was being transformed. New technologies made industrial production more efficient, reducing the number of blue-collar jobs. (This took place well before overseas outsourcing set in.) Almost all of the new positions had professional and managerial titles and required a bachelor's degree. This led more high school graduates—of both genders—to consider college. The midcentury years were also an era of affluence, bringing the suburban explosion, along with discretionary income for new purchases and pleasures. So as baby boomers were reaching their teens, an increasingly popular purchase was higher education. We might add that college was relatively inexpensive then, and much lower as a fraction of middle-class incomes.

Another shift, this one more cultural, fueled the expansion of existing campuses and the creation of new ones. Young people were becoming more independent, and the idea of living away from home seemed both attractive and acceptable. College was an ideal place to stash a segment of the population, under the rationale that they were being prepared for a productive adulthood.

Fast-forward to today. The University of Minnesota makes for an apt application of Kerr's multiversity vision. By our count, it sponsors upward of two hundred centers and institutes, all underwritten by outside funding. Covering subjects ranging across Spirituality and Healing, Hardwood Ecology, Integrative Leadership, Diesel Research, Minnesota Obesity, Animal Health and Safety, Immigration History, and Transdisciplinary Tobacco Use, the institutes at the University of Minnesota offer a good idea of the variety of fields that are able to find support in the age of the multiversity.

The issues addressed by these and other centers certainly deserve research and exploration. Who can be opposed to promoting animal health and combating obesity? But welcoming them onto our campuses has so eclipsed education—most markedly for undergraduates—that our colleges and universities have become complexes without purpose or direction.

It is tempting to say that the coming of the multiversity was all but inevitable. For example, it had become commonplace to contend that knowledge and information were at the center of our economy, so how could colleges and universities stand apart from that trend? The answer is they haven't. Even smaller colleges sought grants, if only because a commitment to research became associated with stature. Hence the argument that occupations in every sphere have become so esoteric that only college-level training can prepare young people for the modern workplace. From this followed the introduction of undergraduate majors in fields like fire science and animation technology.

The expansion didn't stop with vocational training and esoteric research. As multiversities grew, so did their provision of public entertainment, largely in the form of football and basketball, culminating with bowl championships and finalist tournaments. In the 2008–9 season, a total of 93 million seats were filled at college matches, many of them by neither students nor alumni. Not to mention millions more glued to the tube. Fans with no collegiate ties embrace Penn State and Louisville as "their" teams, with whom they identify and cheer on.

As the multiversity expanded, a new breed of educational executive came on the scene. Whereas most of these CEOs had started as professors and held doctoral degrees, they soon found they had administrative talents and used them to climb the hierarchy. Not surprisingly, they are ambitious. The new presidents' records and reputations grow as they are able to point to the kinds of institutes and centers we've cited, plus long lists of grants and contracts, and academic stars they've hired. Hence the bid by Berkeley's chancellor to take over the Los Alamos nuclear facility, 891 miles away in New Mexico. Or the pride of NYU's president as he unveiled plans for a branch of his university in the even more distant sands of Abu Dhabi (6,843 miles away). The modern president is part executive officer, part entrepreneur, with the latter always looking for opportunities. The operative idea is that your institution must always find ways to expand; because if it doesn't, it will surely fall behind. But what multiplies—as in multiversity—are not seminars for freshman, but research centers in mass spectrometry and institutes for transportation systems, which are also magnets for grants and earmarked appropriations.

Leadership might put a brake on much of this administrative excess. After all, all colleges have a structure with at least a titular head. The schools' chancellors and presidents do more than raise funds—they set policy and can create a tone and a direction for an institution. They could stop the mindless growth; they could veto dubious schemes. However, true leadership, which calls for putting the greater good above playing it safe, has become extremely rare among higher education administrators.

Once upon a time, university leaders were seen as sculptors of society; they were national figures, household names, frequently asked to serve on commissions, to comment on significant events, to participate in the public square. Today an average American would be hard-pressed to cite the name of a single college president. The short answer is that hardly any of them have *done* anything memorable, apart perhaps from firing a popular athletic coach.

Twenty-first-century presidents are chiefly technocrats, agile climbers who reach the top without making too many enemies or mistakes. If business leaders get ahead by increasing profits or share value, presidents do it by extending their school's terrain;

like real estate acquisitions and flashy graduate programs. Each night they pray that no football scandal or Ward Churchill will break on their watch, lest it imperil a move to a bigger and better post. The career trajectory of E. Gordon Gee, currently in his second round as head of Ohio State University, is illustrative; he has had six stints heading five universities:

University of West Virginia	1981–1985
University of Colorado	1985–1990
Ohio State University	1990–1997
Brown University	1998–2000
Vanderbilt University	2000–2007
Ohio State University	2007 to present

And Gee has become the best-paid president in public education, courtesy of an adoring board of trustees. In 2009, his package was predicted to exceed $2 million, when bonuses and deferred compensation were included. He also receives an additional several hundred thousand for sitting on corporate boards.

Gordon Gee's frequent rival in the best-paid sweepstakes is Shirley Ann Jackson, who heads Rensselaer, an engineering school that happens to hold an unimpressive 21st place in the *U.S. News & World Report* engineering rankings, an assessment by professional peers. In 2008, her on-campus remuneration totaled $1,598,249. But that was only the beginning. Jackson, a physicist who chaired the Nuclear Regulatory Commission in the Clinton administration, took in another $1,396,632 for directorships at IBM, FedEx, Medtronic, Marathon Oil, Public Service Enterprise, and the New York Stock Exchange. With all this moonlighting, it's hard to see how she gives her day job the attention it requires. Indeed, we wonder why Rensselaer's trustees would even permit their chief executive to sit on *six* outside boards. Or why these firms would choose a director with so many other commitments. In the business world, it's generally agreed that once you hold more than two seats, it's impossible to fathom what's really going on. "I have a lot of energy," was Ms. Jackson's explanation to the *Chronicle of Higher Education.*

It's not surprising that her tenure at Rensselaer has been controversial. Tuition, room and board, and books come to $50,522, one of the highest tabs in the country. But students who choose engineering tend to come from fairly modest backgrounds, so they rely more on loans, and 70 percent of Rensselaer's undergraduates are already in debt. The average loan for the student body, freshmen through seniors, is $30,375; so for those graduating it's likely to be double. We cite these figures since we think something is amiss when a president collects almost $3 million while her students face decades of dunning notices.

We speak so much about money because we believe it subverts leadership. Patrick Callan of the National Center for Public Policy and Higher Education was even more caustic. "We've created a cadre of hired guns, whose economic interests are totally divorced from students and faculty," he said. "It creates a real problem for leadership, and does nothing to help higher education." We agree that it isn't easy to have a conclusive discussion about what is appropriate compensation for a college president. Trustees and regents hire college presidents and make the compensation decisions. What they are looking for is someone they'll feel comfortable with and who speaks to their values. As in the corporate world, a big payout is often seen as reflecting the status of the institution.

But in higher education, it can distort. Here's a case in point. A few years ago some of the trustees at American University, an unexceptional private institution in the District of Columbia, sensed something was amiss about their president, Benjamin Ladner. In fact, most of the board didn't want to know they might have a problem; after all, they had picked him, and to look too deeply would reflect on their own judgment. A report that was eventually commissioned questioned some half a million dollars in expenses, which he charged to the university. Among them, $88,000 for a personal chef; $5,000 for a party for his wife's garden club; $2,513 for a limousine during a two-day sojourn in London; plus $1,381 for an engagement dinner for four for his son. (Featured on the menu: porcini egg custard and lobster bourbon bisque.)

Nor have we seen reports suggesting he felt this sort of spending was out of line. Despite media exposure, as well as student and public outrage, the trustees handed Ladner a $3.7 million severance package, which would eat up the tuitions of 107 American University students. These and other abuses caused Senator Charles Grassley to call them "a poster child for why review and reform are necessary."

We think they are. We don't know if American's new president shares his predecessor's tastes. Still, the trustees are paying him $1,419,339, well above the national average and more than any of the presidents in the Ivy League. As it happens, a near neighbor of his at 1600 Pennsylvania Avenue makes do on $400,000 (plus, like him, a residence). Why is it too much to hope that those who head colleges should regard their work as a public service? When they ask for—or simply accept—$1,419,339, the line begins to dissolve between entitlement and arrogance.

As we noted at the outset, administrative perks contribute to why tuition fees have moved into the stratosphere. When a friend of ours was chosen to head a small liberal arts school, he attended a meeting jocularly called "president's boot camp," a workshop on the nuts and bolts of the job. "Perhaps I was naïve, but I was shocked by how they kept on talking about perks," he later reported. "There was constant one-upping about the size of the presidential residence and whether your car came with a driver."

As it happens, Vartan Gregorian, Gordon Gee's immediate predecessor at Brown, did not have a chauffeured car. During his years in Providence, it was a matter of local legend that he called taxis or even used public transportation. And, unlike many of his peers, he didn't make his salary part of his original negotiations for the job, just asking for what the person he was replacing received. "For a lot of presidents, it's a badge of honor to announce they are the highest paid," he told us. "I'd personally be ashamed." Moreover, he brushed aside overtures from other schools, since he felt that taking the top job called for commitment to the college, say, for as long as a two-term president. When he talks of the qualities most trustees look for in prospective presidents, intellect, Dr. Gregorian believes, is low on the list. "People want fund-raisers," he explained to us, while sitting in the Carnegie Corporation's philanthropy office, which he now heads.

It's become common to muse about a "crisis of leadership," whether in higher education or the nation as a whole. Why, we hear, can't we produce presidents like Franklin Roosevelt or Theodore Roosevelt, or their college counterparts like Charles William Eliot and Robert Maynard Hutchins? We too would like to see courage, inspiration, and imagination at the helm. All too many of our colleges have become rudderless leviathans, taking on any chore that will bring them attention. Equally disquieting is that too few are guided by enunciated principles or a sense of purpose.

Still, it's too easy to issue plaints about a lack of leadership in academic oval offices. The hard fact is that on the modern campus, no one really wants to be led. Every current and former college president we've met has related how every proposal he or she made was greeted by a chorus of no's or simply stone-faced resistance. Add in faculty, trustees, alumni, legislators, and nowadays students, each with their own demands. Indeed, when presidents call for something new, they usually find they have no allies. So it's not surprising that many of them settle for being custodians, along with honing a reputation for diplomacy and fund-raising that will propel them to a higher-ranked campus.

But if, like the elder president Bush, they sometimes find

themselves musing about the "vision thing," we want to offer an immodest proposal. What if colleges and universities were to shed their research components so they could focus on education? All those centers and institutes could more fruitfully function at dedicated facilities like the Howard Hughes and Salk institutes, or at independent think-tanks like the Rand Corporation and the Brookings Institution. At least we wouldn't be hearing complaints from researchers when they are asked to teach undergraduates, and there would be less incentive for universities to keep overproducing PhDs. And while they're at it, why not spin off their medical schools? They have become titanic empires, so concerned with the cutting-edge that they can no longer prepare family-practice physicians. And we might remind ourselves that Princeton is an estimable university, not least in the sciences, and does very well without a medical school. If the leaders of our campuses cannot stop this mushrooming of unnecessary appurtenances, who will?

It has not always been this way. Here's a pantheon of presidents whose portraits we'd like to see mounted in every current incumbent's office. We'll start with *David Starr Jordan,* Stanford's first president, from 1891 to 1916, whose educational vision laid the foundations of a great university. He was also a scholar, trained as an ichthyologist, and traveled to Tennessee to testify for John Scopes in the evolution trial. Yes, he was something of an autocrat. But in his time, many men and women with missions were. In some ways, his model was *Charles William Eliot,* who headed Harvard for four decades, from 1869 to 1909. He used those years to change Harvard from a playground for young gentlemen to a worldwide center of research and scholarship. Think William James and Louis Agassiz. Eliot personally sponsored the doctoral studies of W. E. B. DuBois and an honorary degree for Booker T. Washington. His signal defeat was his attempt to abolish football, which he called "a fight whose strategy and ethics are those of war."

Amherst's *Alexander Meiklejohn* was one of the first champions of liberal education in a literal sense. His trustees abided him from 1913 to 1923, but his efforts to get students thinking proved too much for them. In a college-wide course, students were assigned a volume edited by Upton Sinclair called *The Cry for Justice,* where Wall Street didn't come out well. *Martha Carey Thomas,* who headed Bryn Mawr from 1894 to 1922, not only affirmed that women had intellects, but that they should be inspired to develop their talents. Under her guidance, Bryn Mawr graduates carved out careers as judges, scholars, and physicians, as Katharine Hepburn and Marianne Moore did in acting and poetry. *Robert Maynard Hutchins* led the University of Chicago from 1929 to 1951, introducing its famed "great books" curriculum within a freestanding undergraduate college that gave its students first attention. His valedictory was a book he titled *The University of Utopia.* The title alone showed that twenty-two years at the helm hadn't dampened his educational dreams. The same could be said for that loyal son of John Dewey, *Harold Taylor,* who headed Sarah Lawrence College from 1945 to 1959. Taylor stood up to McCarthyite witch hunts while Harvard and Columbia and Berkeley were supinely cooperating. He always spoke his mind, as to a national educational conference: "The whole educational system has become one massive quiz program with the prizes going to the man with his hand up first."

Is it too much to hope we might again have giants like these on our campuses? We've met a few college presidents who seem to have greatness within them. We'll introduce them in our final chapter. We realize that history can't always repeat itself—underlying conditions change. But we'd like to think that mounting those presidential portraits we proposed would have a small effect. Just possibly, they could stir some of the current crop, when they have a moment alone, to ponder, *Why am I here?*

· 3 ·

CONTINGENT EDUCATION

Some years ago, at a college where Claudia was teaching a non-fiction writing course, she found herself working without an assigned office space. All college teachers require a dedicated corner where they can confer with their students. And Claudia's specialty—journalism training—is particularly dependent on professor-student interactions. Claudia's students bring her their tentative first attempts at reporting. She must show them where they've gone right or wrong and gently steer them onto a successful path. Given the vulnerability of young writers, all of this is best done delicately, and in private. "I have no office space for meeting my students—what can we do about this?" Claudia inquired of the administrator who ran her department.

"There's no space left this term," the administrator declared dismissively, annoyed. "The regular faculty have taken everything."

"I understand," Claudia persisted, "but what are my students to do? This is part of their training."

"Couldn't you meet them in the cafeteria? Or the hallway? There are a couple of lounge chairs by the ladies' room."

That stunned her. Was this person actually suggesting that Claudia confer with her students south of a toilet?

This administrator, an individual who herself enjoyed a large, airy office far from the scent of the lavatory, grew increasingly irritated with Claudia's insistence that her students deserved better. After ten minutes of back and forth, came this: "Listen here, Ms. Dreifus, you're an adjunct! Do you get that? We've got a hundred adjuncts here. I'm busy."

Ah, the pecking order of the university! Claudia—who'd previously spent much of her life as a professional journalist—didn't yet understand her lowly place in this new environment.

Adjuncts belong to a diverse group of teachers called contingents, who are hired to take on chores regular faculty members don't want to do. Their numbers and ratios increase with the size of a university, but since most students now attend larger schools, this raises their chances of getting a contingent education.

As we noted earlier, contingent faculty fall in several tiers.

Instructors and Lecturers. These positions have some security, but are low on status. They receive modest salaries and benefits, and many have multiyear contracts. It is generally understood that they will not move to the tenure track. By and large, they do jobs the higher tiers don't want, like compositions sections or freshman mathematics. Many are faculty spouses.

Visiting Faculty. Here we are not referring to academic or kindred celebrities, who come to grace a campus for outlandish salaries. Rather, they are more likely to be young doctorate holders who cannot find a regular appointment. They fill in for professors on sabbatical or maternity leave. Many have had a succession of such appointments, but they are never asked to stay. They receive health and other benefits, but only for the period they are in residence.

Adjuncts. There are so many it's impossible to get a reliable count. The range runs from respected professionals like lawyers and film producers who teach one evening course (largely because they enjoy it) to gypsy scholars who commute among as many as four campuses in a single week. As we've noted, pay rates are shamefully low. The American Federation of Teachers found the average is about $3,000 per course, which means many get less.

Teaching Assistants. In colleges that have master's and doctoral programs, graduate students are regularly used as cheap teaching labor. Most typically, they run discussion sections in large lecture classes, freeing the professors from personal contact with undergraduates and chores they feel are beneath them. An American Association of University Professors survey of 280 research universities found that together they employed 181,481 teaching assistants, ranging from 5,376 at Berkeley to 202 at the University of Chicago. It's difficult to track down information on what all graduate assistants are paid. Still, we can report that the stipend at Yale, as a school with more resources than most, is about $20,000 for the nine teaching months, plus another $3,500 to survive over the summer. Even for a single person, this is essentially a poverty wage.

At the end of the day, contingents are no more part of the system than an office temp might be, though few modern universities—or, for that matter, many colleges—could function without them. So we're not easy with calling them "faculty," even as they carry the same teaching responsibilities as tenured and tenure track professors.

What contingency is about is money. At Queens College, a branch of the City University of New York, where Andrew teaches political science, for example, the pay is better than average, but the disparities are typical. When students walk into the gleaming building that is Powdermaker Hall, they might see one classroom where a full professor is explaining the economic ideas of the Nation's Founders. He'll earn $116,000 for six classes taught over nine months—$17,000 per course. In the very next room is an adjunct teaching political theory to thirty bright-eyed freshmen. But she gets a flat fee of $4,600, admittedly higher than the national average, but so is the urban cost of living. Moreover, the professor has health insurance, sick days, sabbaticals, and a hefty TIAA-CREF pension. The adjunct's benefits are akin to W. C. Fields's reward in *The Bank Dick*—"a hearty handshake."

This is one of the anomalies of the system. Higher education is probably one of the only sectors of the national workplace where one regularly finds two people with similar credentials, working side by side at comparable jobs, and experiencing such extreme pay gaps. We are not talking here about the skill differentials between an airline pilot and an airport cleaner; adjuncts often perform as well, sometimes better, than the tenured staff.

And there's the respect factor. Contingents are the Rodney Dangerfields of higher education. "Everyone's rude to you; the chair, the tenured, even, at times, the assistant professors," reports Jose Vasquez, a biologist who held adjunct positions at four colleges in Chicago and New York before landing a full-time position. "Plus departmental secretaries, because they are low on the totem pole, but you're still lower."

And yet, as we write this in 2010, the bulk of the undergraduate teaching at our nation's colleges and universities is performed by part-timers, a fact we note in both sorrow and anger. Twenty-first-century freshmen are finding that many, if not most, of their basic classes are likely to be conducted by contingents. Harvard and Yale coat the pill by calling them "teaching fellows." But "fellow" or "assistant," this is not what parents think they're getting for the hundreds of thousands of dollars that an Ivy League education costs. In 1975, the first year the U.S. Department of Education kept statistics in this area, only 43 percent of college teachers were classified as contingents. Today it's nearly 70 percent.

How did this practice become so ubiquitous, anyway?

Ernst Benjamin, the former General Secretary of the American Association of University Professors, told us, "At many schools individual faculty members believed there would be more money for them if they used part-time faculty. But however economically rational it was in their own department, if you did this across the country, it became a problem."

The explosion of contingent instruction has several causes. But we're wary of attributing it chiefly to a bureaucratic desire to hold costs down. Indeed, until endowments started melting, administrations were happy to spend freely across the board, including on the academic side. As we've noted, the paper ratio of professors to students grew, as did top faculty salaries relative to the cost of living.

In fact, the increasing reliance on adjuncts and other transitory teachers arose largely from developments within the permanent faculty. Due to possessing tenure and optional retirement, full professors had come to outnumber those holding associate and assistant rank. As a result, most of the faculty budget was earmarked for the highly paid people at the top, so less was left to bring in new junior faculty, especially assistant professors. The generous bestowal of tenure, at least for those lucky enough to be on the track, also distorted the payroll. Faculty with lifetime appointments have stayed on and on. Moreover, they are generally given annual raises, in the name of comity. Hence the hiring of contingents, who underwrite these increments for full professors.

Even smaller colleges now want to talk about how their professors are publishing and giving conference papers. With so many faculty taking time away from teaching, more visitors and part-timers were brought in to ensure that necessary courses were given. In a similar quest for status, colleges recast themselves as universities in order to attract graduate students and award advanced degrees. After all, academic reputations come from offering research seminars and supervising dissertations. In consequence, fewer professors had the time—indeed, the desire—to teach the undergraduate classes that had once been their usual load. Adjuncts took their place, especially at the introductory level.

Accompanying the search for status was an increasing air of loftiness, often bordering on arrogance. More professors felt they could simply say no, they wouldn't teach underclass courses, or indeed any course outside their sub-specialty. At many elite universities, even the core curriculum and large lecture classes are handed over to the contingent personnel.

Supply and demand interact. In particular, a growing supply can subtly spur demand. The growing army of contingents made it easier for regular faculty to do less work, or at least take on only the tasks they chose. Indeed, all these transitory adjuncts and temporary part-timers had been nurtured by the very professors whose erstwhile classes they were teaching. And here administrators played a role. Just as in the name of efficiency they had replaced cafeteria staffs with outside contractors, instructors paid only for a term at a time made economic sense. We'd only add that in doing this, they didn't encounter objections from the full-time faculty.

Ironically, as we write this in the midst of the recession that began in the fall of 2008, there may be a slight dip in the number of contingents on campus. With the budget stringencies created by the financial crisis, contingents were the first to be trimmed from the payroll. However, when you fire a contingent, you cancel a course. In the University of California system, students are finding they can't get the classes they need for their majors and degrees. The schools are actually planning on shrinking their undergraduate enrollment, though there are few plans to trim tenured professors. We have yet to find senior faculty acknowledging that they bear some responsibility for this.

Adjunct teachers, of course, take many forms. We've picked two, from different parts of the country, to show the faces of some men and women who are providing the bulk of undergraduate education.

Matt Williams lives in the Akron area and does most of his teaching at the local university bearing that name. Like some of the contingent class, particularly those who instruct in English courses, he teaches with only a master's degree. Last year, he told us, he taught twelve different classes at two colleges. He also picks up extra income by writing press releases for companies and delivering automobiles. His wife has chosen to stay at home with their two young children. Their take-home income must be significantly below $30,000 since his family qualifies for and receives Medicaid.

Williams is—or was—politically conservative. He grew up around a university; his father taught electrical engineering. "I'm about the last guy you'd think would be fighting for a union," he said during an interview, laughing. It's the numbers that radicalized him. In the course he teaches on public speaking, there's a unit on how to address social issues. "I've asked my students, 'How much do you think I make?' Their mouths flew open when I said it works out to $8.65 an hour. They were absolutely unaware. One of the things I've started to do—and urge others to do also—is put on the top of their course syllabus, 'This class is being taught by a professor who earns $8.65 an hour.'"

The way he's calculated his personal economics, "If I could work doing the same thing as a full-time lecturer, I would make $32,000 a year. If I were an associate professor of communications, I would earn $50,000." Of course, to become an associate professor on tenure track, he'd need at least a PhD. Matt Williams is too busy running from one job to another to even consider returning to school. Besides, in the area he wants to teach—undergraduate communications and speech—the courses are more and more being left to part-timers with a master's degree in Fine Arts. As the writer P. D. Lesko, who publishes the web magazine *Adjunct Nation*, jokes, "MFA really means 'More Faculty Adjuncts.'"

Matt Williams is torn about his future. He's joined the New Faculty Majority, a national coalition of adjuncts that is not a labor union per se, but a kind of Internet chat room where people can meet and exchange ideas. By all accounts, he's skilled and committed in the classroom, encouraging students to think for themselves. Even so, he's close to abandoning the academic world. "I need to get out of what I'm doing right now before I paint myself into a corner," he says. "I have corporate experience. It's getting to the point where my obligation to my family is superseding everything else."

Even if Matt Williams could go back to school for the PhD, many years of adjuncting wouldn't count as valuable classroom experience. Rather, for most, it's a black mark. This was borne out by an informal survey Angelo Gene Monaco, the vice president for human resources at the University of Akron, performed. Out of curiosity, he surveyed sixty heads of departments at a sample of midwestern colleges. Only three told him they'd even consider hiring a contingent for a full-time post. Monaco created quite a stir at the 2008 meeting of the College and University Professional Association for Human Resources when he declared: "We've helped create a highly educated part of the working poor."

Angelo Gene Monaco could be speaking of Deborah Louis. In the 1960s, she wrote a real book, a history of the civil rights movement called *And We Are Not Saved*, which was published by Doubleday. She attended prestigious schools and has a PhD. But, as she had young children, she opted for part-time teaching. "I had three daughters and I needed to be available to them," she told us. "I also wanted to consult for community organizations."

Long since divorced, she now earns her daily bread doing adjunct teaching at Eastern Kentucky University and Asheville-Buncombe Technical Community College in North Carolina. As an adjunct, she's never had a year where she's earned more than $40,000; many years have been much, much leaner.

But Louis is still drawn to research. So at Asheville-Buncombe, she distributed a questionnaire to her fellow adjuncts. Among her findings, which she reported to the *Chronicle of Higher Education*:

- About two-thirds of those who answered her questionnaire were "women who have children or dependent adults at home and whose pay, whether alone or with a partner's earnings, are essential to their households."

- Half taught three or more courses—in other words, a full load. She had one respondent who was teaching twelve classes.

- Less than half felt they were "respected by the salaried faculty members and administrators or that they were perceived as part of the campus community."

None of this astonished Louis; it's her own story. Nor does it surprise Alison Gopnick, a psychologist at Berkeley. "If ever there was a women's issue in the academy, this is it," she told us. "Adjuncting is where the so-called Mommy Track is. A lot of women think they can have families and stay in the game by adjuncting. They get trapped there."

Age and time also traps them. Vagabonding from job to job isn't so terrible when you're young, but it takes its toll on the part-timers as they get older. When we last spoke with Deborah Louis, she said she was trying to cobble together a livelihood by teaching sixteen "distance" courses. Online teaching, she said, was tougher than face-to-face instruction, because, if you do it seriously, "you never get a break from it. You almost sleep with your computer."

Though she enjoyed the students she'd encountered at the community colleges, monitoring an army of distance learners might be easier on her, in the long run, than shuttling between campuses. When we inquired about her health insurance, Dr. Louis chuckled. She'll be eligible for Medicare in about a year. That's an adjunct's health insurance.

Once upon a time, these adjunct teachers were graduate students—which is where the exploitation usually begins. While pursuing higher degrees, they were part of a nationwide cohort of as many as 250,000 teaching assistants. Their use runs pretty much from 55 percent of all instructional personnel at Penn State to about 40 percent at Brown. Higher education couldn't function without them. Even respected liberal arts colleges like Wellesley and Macalester bring in some graduate students to fill in as adjuncts.

At the research universities, it's the graduate students who mostly handle the "sections" of the large lecture classes, although many are now assigned courses of their own. And at most universities, the teaching assistants are simply put in front of students, sink or swim. Kindergarten teachers get more preparation in how to teach than graduate assistants at our universities. True, many universities have "teaching centers" where novices can get pointers and coaching, but they are generally unvisited. As a student wrote in the *Yale Daily News*, "the University does not have any centralized system for preparing graduate student teaching fellows to assist a professor or lead a class, and there is no official remedy for dealing with the problems that may arise throughout the semester if a teaching fellow is unprofessional or unprepared."

So teaching the teachers is mostly left to the few professors who really care. Harvard's Michael Sandel treats his section assistants as if they are themselves in a seminar. They meet weekly to consider not only substantive topics but also devices for orchestrating discussions and getting everyone involved. In short, Sandel defined his job as teaching his graduate assistants how to teach. We watched Carl Wieman doing the same thing in his "Physics for Engineers" class at the University of Colorado—and it was inspiring. One hitch, which we'll be considering later, is that not all senior professors are good teachers themselves, so they don't have any useful advice to pass on. At best, observing them might provide lessons in what not to do.

There are also limits to what tutelage can achieve in an institution where cost-cutting is paramount. A telling story came to us from Jose Vasquez, the NYU biologist, who, a few years back, coordinated graduate science teaching assistants at a public university in the Chicago area: "A lot of the graduate assistants came from abroad and their English simply wasn't good enough for them to be in front of American students," he recalled. "It was horrible for the students, who complained they couldn't understand their instructors. I went to the administration and said, 'You've got to give these TAs six months of intensive English before putting them into a classroom. They said, 'That's too expensive.' This really bothered me because the students were taking the science classes for medical school admission. This hurt them."

At the risk of sounding nativist, we have to report that students everywhere told us that foreign graduate students, particularly in mathematics and the sciences, are a problem. Because few Americans are opting for advanced study in these fields, our universities go to China, Russia, and India not just to fill up their seminars but for teachers of calculus and physics to undergraduates. That's a stopgap when they speak English. But if they can't, it's a disaster.

Meanwhile, graduate fellows across the country have attempted to unionize in a quest to better their conditions. At Yale and Cornell, such moves have been resisted by the administration; at NYU, the university attempted to break the union. Until recently, the National Labor Relations Board has held that teaching assistants at private institutions aren't legally workers but more like apprentices learning a craft. So they have had an uphill fight to gain representation and collective bargaining. But in 2010, the panel's membership was reconfigured, and that ruling may change. (At public universities, the right to unionize depends on state laws. In Wisconsin and Michigan, the legislatures have been sympathetic. Not surprisingly, in Idaho and Louisiana, they have not.)

In more golden years, when faculties were expanding almost exponentially, most PhDs could expect a promising starting job. Off in their future was the life of the mind, at passable pay, with plenty of leisure time. No longer. The story can be told in two recent figures. Between 2005 and 2007 American universities awarded 101,009 doctoral degrees. The number of new assistant professorships created in those years: 15,820. Even if we allow that half of new PhDs take jobs outside teaching, there are at least three aspiring scholars for each academic opening. Despite graduate students' poor chances on the academic market, senior professors have a vested interest in new graduate students coming in: They not only help with teaching—the number of graduate students that professors have working under them is a metric of their own prestige.

Given the implications of these figures, we think that senior professors should be having conversations with first-year graduate students that go something like: "In all honesty, you have less than a one-in-three chance of getting a full-time job as an academic. Your only motive for pursuing your doctorate should be your own intellectual development."

But given professors' self-interest, such frankness is likely to be rare. Nor are first-rank research schools like Berkeley and Yale the only ones bestowing doctoral mantles. The list has expanded to 280, burgeoned by regional state universities hoping to raise their status. Among them are Florida Atlantic, Georgia Southern, Eastern Michigan, and Middle Tennessee universities, which are all now adding to the national overproduction of doctorates.

Not so very long ago even a Georgia Southern University could send its PhDs to fill faculty positions at colleges in the region. Now those schools are only advertising for adjuncts. There's a glut of PhDs on the labor market and the colleges are quite willing to take advantage of it.

What college administrators need to understand is that some educational practices may be counterproductive. Paul D. Umbach at North Carolina State University studied 21,000 faculty members at 148 colleges and found that at schools using lots of part-timers, the regular teaching staff put in fewer hours of preparation than their peers at institutions where adjuncts were rare. He went on to suggest that the presence of so many part-timers makes the regular faculty insecure, which "translates into lower levels of commitment and performance." As more and more adjuncts are brought in, even tenured professors begin to feel increasingly beleaguered. That's one interpretation. We'd like to suggest another one—that at schools with a large contingent teaching staff, some of the full-timers may just feel: Hey, let the adjuncts do it!

Another study, by Audrey J. Jaeger of North Carolina State University and M. Kevin Eagan Jr. at UCLA, mined the transcripts of some 30,000 undergraduates enrolled in four public universities in the Southeast. They found a strong relationship between dropout rates and having contingent faculty teaching basic freshmen courses. They also looked at community college students in California and found that when students were taught by contingents their odds of going on to four-year colleges decreased.

Yet what amazed us is how many contingents are actually effective, a miracle considering the conditions under which they work. Indeed, at nearly every school we visited, when we asked students for the name of a favorite professor, they frequently mentioned a contingent. Jonathan Meltzer, a Harvard undergraduate, echoed the views of many when he told us, "Professors I have had, who are not tenured, are sometimes—not always—more motivated by teaching, more interested in making sure their students are enjoying their classes, probably because they feel that will sort of help them down the line. But in general maybe it's also because they are closer in age and can more easily interact with the students."

At the University of Maryland, Baltimore County, Bradley Walker's favorite professor was an adjunct. UMBC is not all that far from Washington and it sometimes gets interesting part-timers who have practical experience in government. Walker told us, "The knee-jerk reaction would be to say that part-time professors are the worst professors, but here I would take exception to that. There's a part-time professor who works at the CIA and teaches a class and he consistently ranks as one of the best professors among students."

Both of us have served as adjuncts at different times in our careers. It has occurred to us that some contingents love teaching so much that they'll do it with dignity and care, regardless of low pay. It's sad that their passion for the classroom is so readily exploited.

We all fill our homes with inexpensive products that are fabricated overseas at Third World wages. At this point, we can't outsource History 101 to be taught in Bangalore. (Although, as we'll show in a later chapter, something akin to that is already being done.) What we do instead is hire our own citizens and give them Third World pay. What is ironic—no, it's tragic—is that these bright men and women are so anxious to ply their profession that they are willing to toil in the academic counterparts of sweatshops and vegetable fields.

We wish we could end this chapter on an upbeat note. But it's clear that higher education knows that low-cost labor is there. This can already be seen in two-year colleges, many of which have found ways to operate essentially without faculties. Florida Keys Community College has eighteen permanent professors, who then bring in 123 adjuncts to teach the bulk of its courses. Missouri's Moberly College makes do with only three professors, who recruit 254 adjuncts and instructors. Administrators at four-year schools may well be paying visits to see how they do it.

Nor is this race to the bottom finished. At some schools, contingents, cheap as they are, are seen as still too costly. Several of the University of Pennsylvania's freshmen sections at the Wharton School are supervised by upperclass undergraduates. Yale has a shortage of graduate teaching assistants and there has been talk, as we write, to train upperclassmen and women to serve as "section leaders." Such plans are already afoot at NYU, where a pre-medical student told us of undergraduate section leaders in science courses. "They pay them a little something," she said.

PART 2

IDEALS AND ILLUSIONS

· 4 ·

THE GOLDEN DOZEN

The gathering was one often seen during college application seasons. Present were parents and high school juniors at an upscale suburban high school. The town was in a verdant corner of New York's Westchester County. It could easily have been Winnetka or Bloomfield Hills or even Beverly Hills. The featured speaker was an admissions officer from an Ivy college, one known for accepting only a minute fraction of its applicants.

The traveling admissions officer began with a killer opening: "Let me be brutally frank. Most of you shouldn't even bother applying to my school. At best, we'll be accepting only one or two of you. For one thing, we look for regional diversity when we build a class. So, no matter how good your record—high SATs, editor of the newspaper—the odds are still against you."

She then turned to what seemed a well-rehearsed statement. "But you know, there are many excellent colleges in this country where you can get just as fine an education as at high-profile schools like Yale or Duke or Williams. There's Davidson, Carleton, and Grinnell, if you're looking for a small liberal arts college. Vanderbilt, Emory, and Washington outside St. Louis are excellent universities. Moreover, for many of you, getting accepted at one of them can be a reasonable expectation."

These remarks rankled. Of course these parents—neurologists, trial lawyers, corporate consultants—were aware of Carleton and Grinnell. To their minds, schools like that were beside the point. They'd moved too far up the social ladder to send their Jason or Jennifer to an off-brand school. Their hard-won status demanded something Ivy. Nothing less would do.

What are the ultra-desired schools that inspire such fierce—and elitist—devotion? There are twelve that recur again and again on the list of those parents who demand the very best. We'll be calling them the Golden Dozen. Of course, it's not an "official" list. There is no body, public or private, authorized to make such a choice. But they are not just our personal favorites. We've been listening to parents all across the country, and there's an eerie unanimity. The twelve schools we identify are not just one region's selection, but one that will be echoed by a successful urologist in Dubuque, the leading banker in Tulsa, and a top tax attorney in either of the Charlestons.

Here they are, the eight that make up the Ivy League, plus four more of comparable status:

Harvard	Cornell
Yale	Penn
Princeton	Stanford
Dartmouth	Duke
Brown	Amherst
Columbia	Williams

The Golden Dozen! For many parents, the stern fact is that there's a wide chasm between them and whichever school might come next. Rice, Northwestern, Wesleyan, and Swarthmore—all truly excellent institutions—simply do not command the recognition that aspiring parents want. This is seen most vividly with those whose offspring don't win a Dozen billet. When among acquaintances, they find themselves stammering that Earlham College really has an excellent internship program, which is what their Sarah wanted.

But what exactly are these parents embracing when they anxiously seek admission to the Golden Dozen for their children? Do these schools really represent the "best" educations in the nation? And what does "the best" mean anyway?

It's easy to assume that the quality of teaching at both Harvard and Penn, or the priorities at Williams, are pinnacles of educational success. But how much of that assumption is based on aura and how much in reality is a question that rarely gets asked.

In 2009, after the colleges and applicants had made their choices, the Dozen had slightly over 15,000 freshmen arriving for orientation, or just under 1 percent of the national entering class. (The Dozen's total may increase somewhat, since some of the schools are talking about expanding their intakes.) We should add that for Cornell and Penn, we have counted only their arts and science students, since both schools have large vocational programs. A Cornell degree in hotel administration, or one in nursing from Penn, doesn't confer the status usually associated with the Dozen.

Once upon a time, most of those freshman came via a very particular route—the private day or boarding school. Nowadays, though those schools are still in business, they no longer have guaranteed access. At Groton, in a recent year, only a third of its graduates ended up at Dozen schools. While that fraction might cheer most college counselors, for many of the parents who invested in Groton it's another story. When their offspring end up at Hobart, Dickinson, and Georgetown, it looks a lot like downward mobility. The parents at the meeting that opened this chapter were clearly prosperous, and could pay the full fee at any of the Dozen colleges. But what also needs noting is that families in that bracket are no longer a small minority. In 1982, only 3 percent of all American households took in over $100,000 a year. By 2008, the most recent figures at this writing and using same-value dollars, fully 26 percent of all families were in the six-figure tier. Even with the recent recession, they would provide quite a few full payers. So the ascent of more families to the top tiers has bulked up the demand for Dozen places, while the supply has hardly changed.

There would be less grief about this if this middle-class constituency were willing to bestow the coveted honorific on just-below schools like Northwestern and Wesleyan, or Swarthmore and Vanderbilt. But they aren't. Somehow, the chasm separating the Dozen from all others stays as wide and deep as ever.

Of course, the Golden Dozen schools are more than status symbols. Amherst, Dartmouth, Williams, and Brown are gorgeous environments and often home to dedicated teachers. Columbia vibrates from the artistic and intellectual energy of New York City. Duke is a good jumping-off point for a medical career, if that's what Jennifer wants—their medical school looks favorably at Duke graduates at admission time. Stanford, the only member of the Dozen west of the Mississippi, has a campus so elegant you might think you're in San Simeon.

That said, the well-known undergraduate instruction is, at best, spotty at the two biggest Ivy brands—Harvard and Yale. Both are basically research universities; most of the senior professors are focused on their scholarly projects, and undergraduate teaching just isn't a priority. This seems to have long been true. At least forty years ago, when computer guru Esther Dyson was a Harvard undergrad, her father, the famed physicist Freeman Dyson, admonished her for essentially majoring in the *Harvard Crimson* and not her coursework. "Dad, we're not here for those classes," she sagely replied. "We're here to meet each other."

In fact, the mediocrity of Harvard undergraduate teaching is an open secret of the Ivy League. So why exactly are parents so eager for their children to attend these schools? We'll acknowledge that even high-striving parents want their children to end up as happy and cultured adults. Still, there's a catchment of Americans—we won't hazard how many—who, above everything, want their children to be *successful*. And the point of the Dozen, perhaps above all else, is to loft their graduates upward as other colleges cannot. Parents may grant that you can get as good an education at Macalester as at Harvard, perhaps even better. Yet for them, the Dozen are seen as a launching pad, from which offspring can be propelled into the nation's elite. If all goes according to plan, in the years ahead you will be able to tell acquaintances that your daughter has just become a partner at Sullivan & Cromwell and your son was recently named chief of urology at the Cleveland Clinic. That's what Princeton and Dartmouth are not so secretly selling. But, we wondered, are they delivering on that assurance?

When it comes to gauging the success of Golden Dozen graduates, it's hard to find solid information. As a start, we decided to look at an institution that represents the next hurdle after college. Our choice was Harvard Law School, since most people will agree it ranks either first or second. (Yale, which we also looked at, tops a lot of lists.) We're not saying everyone wants to become a lawyer, nor is it the only route to success. But we thought, why not let Harvard Law tell us how it ranks undergraduate colleges? Of course, they don't do that in a numeric way; still, their admissions decisions over the years might reveal a few patterns.

We'll take a moment here to note that Harvard declines to make this information public. So we'd like to thank some Cambridge friends, who provided us with lists of the colleges represented in the seven classes that entered from 2002 through 2008.

So here's a summary of what we found. The not-so-big surprise was that almost five hundred of its successful applicants—499, in fact—out of the 3,714 admitted in this period, were already in

Cambridge. The admission office's official story is that candidates from Harvard's own undergraduate college are judged by the same criteria as everyone else. So if they finish with the most acceptances, well ahead of the next contender, which perhaps predictably was Yale, it's just that they were objectively the best. We won't argue, since we have no counter-evidence.

After Yale, in descending order and relative to their size, came nine more of the Golden Dozen: Stanford, Amherst, Columbia, Cornell, Duke, Brown, Dartmouth, and Williams. (Penn, as we'll see, is several rungs behind.) During these seven years, the Golden Dozen were allotted 1,785 of Harvard Law School's 3,714 seats, or 48 percent of the total. This had to mean the other 52 percent, the 1,929 remaining places, were spread among another 298 schools. (A similar analysis of Yale's law school found even more seats—54 percent—going to Dozen graduates.)

The table on the next page lists forty schools that had at least five acceptances. The numbers in parentheses are their seven-year totals for actual admissions. But colleges vary considerably in size. Whereas Amherst's 38 admissions came from a seven-year pool of 2,860 graduates, NYU's 39 were drawn from approximately 32,870, over ten times as many. So we contrived an index that adjusts each school's admissions to its total graduates. By this measure, Harvard still came in first, with the highest acceptance-to-pool ratio, which we scored as 1000.

Even at the top, there's a pecking order. A graduate of Princeton (index: 467) is twice as likely to be accepted as someone from Williams (228). On the other hand, the gap between Duke (277) and Brown (272) is negligible. So Harvard Law's admissions confirm that the Dozen (or at least eleven of them) have a perceptible edge over everyone else. Excellent schools like Emory (69) and Northwestern (84) are very visibly behind. And if we agree that Carleton offers just as good an education as Amherst, it doesn't do nearly as well by Harvard Law's judgment: Amherst (340) sent six times as many of its graduates as Carleton (53).

HOW HARVARD LAW SCHOOL RATES THE COLLEGES

Undergraduate Colleges of 3,714 Accepted Applicants, 2002–2008
(Index takes account of size of colleges' graduating classes. Top College = 1000.)

Harvard (499)	1000
Yale (259)	685
Princeton (144)	467
Stanford (166)	340
Amherst (38)	340
Columbia (118)	315
Cornell (117)	282
Duke (98)	277
Brown (114)	272
Dartmouth (74)	261
Williams (33)	228
Rice (46)	203
Swarthmore (19)	195
Pomona (18)	178
Georgetown (75)	162
U/Penn (125)	160
Chicago (34)	104
Brandeis (23)	102
Barnard (16)	94
Wellesley (15)	94
Northwestern (47)	84
MIT (27)	84
Vanderbilt (29)	74
Bowdoin (9)	74
Emory (30)	69
Middlebury (12)	69
Notre Dame (38)	66
Washington/St. Louis (30)	66
Wesleyan (13)	66
U/C Berkeley (113)	61
Carleton (7)	53
Howard (19)	51
U/Virginia (44)	48
UCLA (82)	41
U/Michigan (59)	36
U/Texas (85)	36
Brigham Young (65)	33
NYU (39)	28
U/North Carolina (27)	25
USC (28)	25

And then there's what we can only call the Penn Problem.
Among those in the know, the University of Pennsylvania's undergraduate college is thought of as the Fredo Corleone of its league.
Yes, there's a venerable name there, but not much else. Parents
are constantly complaining about its large classes and the fact
that some of the teaching is being done by other undergraduates.
It ranks sixteenth in the Harvard Law admissions derby, below
un-Ivied Georgetown and Pomona. (It was also well behind in
the Dozen on the Yale Law list.) Penn might argue that its large
Wharton business cohort freely chooses finance over the law, and
we're sure that many do. That's why we removed them from our
Penn pool and limited it to liberal arts graduates. While in raw
numbers 125 admissions may seem substantial, the truth is that
Penn has close to 10,000 undergraduates, as many as a mid-rank
state campus. With that enrollment, it can't give its students the
intensive attention expected at a Dozen school. It has seventeen
students for each of its professors, which means its classes are
larger than at Brown, where the ratio is 1:13, or Princeton and
Yale, which have 1:10. Still, as long as the University of Pennsylvania has stronger name recognition than, say, Brandeis or Rice,
there will be plenty of parents willing to pay its hefty tab for what
Harvard and Yale law schools regard as a middling product.

From another standpoint, Harvard casts a wide and democratic
net in its admissions. During the seven-year period, it accepted
candidates from fully 310 colleges, many of them quite unassuming, if not obscure. Here's a sampling: Pacific Lutheran, Eastern
Kentucky, Oral Roberts, Valdosta State, Northern Iowa, Colorado School of Mines, Truman State University, Valparaiso College, Southern Oregon, and Wittenberg College. This list suggests
that all applications are opened and read, with no prejudgments
about their source. Even so, this count can be deceptive. Among
the 310 schools, 125 had merely one admission in the seven years,
and another 71 had only two or three, which still means that in
most years these 196 had none at all.

So Harvard Law basically plays both sides of the street. On one side, it reserves close to half its places for students from twelve selective colleges. This makes a kind of sense. Those candidates were validated earlier by the Dozen's admissions offices, and so can be seen as relatively risk-free. Moreover, four years at these highly selective schools will ease the cultural transition into three more at Cambridge.

The other half of Harvard Law's classes—the 1,929 applicants from 298 other schools—present a rather different picture. Students from Valdosta, Valparaiso, and Southern Oregon may have done their bachelor's work at inauspicious colleges, but they are now being given a second shot at elite careers. Upon graduating from law school, most employers (admittedly, not all) will overlook their having started in rural Georgia or agrarian Indiana. So though half of Harvard's admissions reflect advantages already accrued, the other half enables an important professional stratum to renew itself. Indeed, this practice started a century ago, when Harvard admitted a young City College graduate from New York named Felix Frankfurter, whom they retained on their faculty until he was appointed to the U.S. Supreme Court.

In the Harvard Law derby, Princeton ranked third on the preferred list. So one obvious thing its degree can do is position a person for a top law school and whatever comes afterward. Of course, it hardly needs saying that getting into Princeton isn't easy. In recent years, nine out of ten of its applicants have received rejection letters. Nor do we need to reiterate why so many want their children to secure a Princeton pedigree. Once its degree becomes part of your identity, it is generally assumed it will put you—and keep you—well ahead of the pack, that the four years spent on its campus will still be reaping dividends forty years later. This is a school that in recent years has reported it spends $113,000 a year on each of its students, one of the highest per capita allocations in the nation. For this investment alone, a lot is expected of its graduates.

In fact, Princeton's principal reason for being is often affirmed in its presidents' speeches and recurs in fund-raising campaigns. Princeton, we are told on its website, "prepares students for leadership roles." Once more: it aims to "produce leaders in their career fields and community." Again: "Princeton's civic mission is to educate national leaders."

How far does Princeton deliver on this promise? In our own understanding, leadership reveals itself in two ways. One is by inspiring people to rally behind you, whether in local or national politics, a business enterprise, or a military unit. It's not just having a title, but how you mobilize a following and what you do with your position once there. Some Princeton graduates become this kind of public figure. With over 80,000 names on its living alumni rolls, it would be surprising, if not shocking, if so large a pool didn't produce people of stature. James Madison and Woodrow Wilson head its historic list. Ralph Nader and Donald Rumsfeld are also on it. So are self-made entrepreneurs like Meg Whitman of eBay and Jeff Bezos of Amazon.

Another group of leaders consists of men and women who, as was said, are "leaders in their career fields." Here what is wanted is a distinctive contribution, one that gains respectful recognition, whether in your own time or later. Thus one can be a leader in the arts and sciences, or as an attorney or physician who extends a profession's frontiers. Princetonian James Stewart was a leader in his art, as Eugene O'Neill and F. Scott Fitzgerald were in theirs.

To find out how Princeton measures in producing both kinds of leaders, we selected a sample of its graduates for close analysis. The group consists of the 934 now-living men and women who entered as Class of 1973 freshmen or joined it later on. We chose this particular cohort because, first, it was of manageable size to study, yet also large enough to be a reliable sample. Second, it was the first class with women and a relatively sizable black representation, since 1969 was the year that applications from women were first accepted and a decision was made to bring in more students of African origin. Third, and most relevant for our purposes, its members have reached their mid-fifties, and were old enough to have achieved much of what they would do in their lives. We have examined all the material on the class available in Princeton's archives, as well as other sources. Additionally, we have interviewed some of its members.

We started with Princeton's avowal that its mission is to "educate national leaders." By this criterion, we must report that none of the 934 has served in cabinet or sub-cabinet positions, in either congressional chamber, as a federal judge or financial official, or as chief executive of a national corporation. The closest is a career ambassador, who was posted to Panama and Bosnia. Four have held positions at the state level: a one-term secretary of state in Arizona; a judge in Chillicothe, Ohio; a member of the Arkansas legislature; plus a Texas assistant attorney general. The only international figures were Jorge Castaneda, who served as Mexico's foreign secretary during Vincente Fox's administration, and Lisa Halaby, who wed the King of Jordan and has remained active in humanitarian causes.

As might be expected, many of the members gravitated toward the professions. But most have had modest careers. While there were quite a few academics, relatively few made it to leading colleges or universities. More were at places like the University of Akron and Western Missouri State than Harvard or Johns Hopkins. There were many lawyers, but only a handful became partners at elite firms; few of its physicians were at major medical centers. On the business side, one member became editor of *Fortune*'s China edition; another heads the Bronfman Citrus company's branch in Qhongqing, and a third rose to be treasurer of Coca-Cola, the highest corporate title we could find. One woman, Helen Zia, was an editor of *Ms.* magazine.

For a way to quantify the mark class members had made, we went to *Who's Who in America*, which lists men and women who have noteworthy careers. For all its quirks, it's probably the best single index we have of personal distinction. Of the 934 living graduates and non-graduates, a total of 26 are in that volume. Most prominent are Georgia Nugent, the president of Kenyon College; Marcia Vetrocq, the editor of *Art in America*; Deborah Leff, the director of the John F. Kennedy Library; Lizbeth Cohen, chair of the Harvard history department; Page Allen, a Santa Fe artist; Barbara Weinstein, a history professor at NYU and former president of the American Historical Association; and Annalyn Swan and her husband, Mark Stevens, who are Pulitzer Prize–winning biographers. Using *Who's Who* as a guide, 2.8 percent of the class meets this test of national leadership. From where we sit, we find that figure disappointing, but not surprising. After all, we have argued that the reputations of Golden Dozen colleges are inflated. We suspect the proportion would be similar at others in the group like Williams and Yale. Harvard graduates in fact score considerably higher because more of them display that elusive quality called "brilliance."

This is a good place to note that the women in the Class of 1973 turned out considerably more distinctive than the men. By graduation, they represented 18 percent of its rolls. Yet they were 26 percent of those awarded Highest Honors, and 28 percent of elections to Phi Beta Kappa. Nor did they stop there. In later life, they accounted for 35 percent of those listed in *Who's Who in America*, more than twice the ratio attained by the men. And in our view, their contributions were more distinctive. For example, Robin Herman took what she learned from integrating Princeton to become the first woman staff sports writer at the *New York Times*.

On a more mundane side, we're sure that Princeton graduates ended up earning more than those from Vaparaiso College or Southern Oregon. It would be strange if they didn't. Here the best information we could obtain came from a questionnaire that was sent to all members of the class in connection with its 35th reunion, which was held in 2008. They were asked about things like children, hobbies, and extramarital escapades (30 percent said yes to the last). There was also a question on personal income.

But before reporting the results, we should add that only a third—312 out of 934—of the class list returned responses. There's a sociological rule of thumb for surveys like this, which posits that less-successful graduates are not as likely to reply. This said, the median income for the men who responded was $175,000, while for women it was $115,000. We regard the men's figure as surprisingly modest for graduates of an elite college who have reached their mid-fifties. Nor do we need to note that *median* means that of the men, half said they made under $175,000.

We hear that Princeton alumni are deeply loyal and harbor a lifelong love for their alma mater. Here, too, we can only report on the class we've studied. The test comes during the fund-raising season. We examined participation and donations for six recent years, 2004 through 2009. Again, using the 934 extant members of the class, we found that less than half—in fact, 48 percent—sent in contributions. And the other 52 percent? As every alumnus knows, calls come routinely from class agents. Their refrain is basically, even if you have other giving priorities, please send a symbolic check, if only to bolster our participation rate. Why, we wondered, do over half resist sending even a token ten dollars?

Another implied Princeton premise has been not only that its graduates will have ascending careers, but that they will be able to pass that status to their offspring. This hasn't happened, at least with the class we studied. In recent years, Princeton has been rejecting over half—about 60 percent—of its legacy applicants, not so much from a desire to limit alumni children, but because their records don't measure up. A list we obtained showed that only 120 members of the class had children who had also gone there. If something like a 60 percent rate holds for the Class of 1973, it could mean that another 180 had children who applied and were turned down. (No one confessed this in the reunion letters.) The reunion reports mentioned only three as accepted by other Golden Dozen schools, two by Harvard and one by Cornell.

Still, there's a bright side. That so many of the class's children are ending up at less prepossessing schools bodes well for democracy. It tells us that what might have been their progeny's places are going to more talented applicants, often from less established homes. Most visibly, current Princeton classes are now about 14 percent Asian, few of whom are likely to have alumni parents.

We're sure the Princetonians of the Class of 1973 are all good citizens who vote and pay their taxes, maintain their homes and neighborhoods, and take part in local affairs. But Princeton says it expects more than that. It's supposed to produce a stream of Meg Whitmans, Ralph Naders, and Woodrow Wilsons, plus a scattering of Scott Fitzgeralds and Eugene O'Neills. Greater resources are poured into Princeton on the premise—and promise—that most of its graduates will develop distinctive lives and recognized careers. The alumni we've come to know seem like pleasant people, but on the whole, few of them have been making history. We suppose it could be argued that some Princeton graduates could have more modest aspirations. That may be estimable. But that's not the prime purpose of a college that prides itself on its selectivity and its skill in identifying young people of unusual talent and potential.

Hence our question: would the Republic be discernibly different if Princeton's endowments were put to other uses? And how can we ensure the "best education" for our children? To better answer that question, we turn next to some thoughts on the remarkably underappreciated aspect of higher education: good teaching.

· 5 ·

TEACHING: GOOD, GREAT, ABYSMAL

"The colonel's lady and Judy O'Grady are sisters under their skins." Rudyard Kipling's whimsy occurred to us during our visits to two colleges, Harvard and Oregon State University. On first glance, they couldn't be farther apart; indeed, 2,578 miles separate Corvallis and Cambridge. Harvard accepts only 8 percent of its applicants, while Oregon State says yes to 84 percent who submit a form. In recent years, Harvard has been budgeting $125,684 for each of its students; Oregon State makes do with $29,880. There are similar disparities in faculty salaries, graduate school admissions, and how their degrees are regarded. But what they have in common—and connects them with many other colleges— is the teaching their students receive. All in all, it's pretty poor. What we saw and heard at Harvard and Oregon State is emblematic of a pervasive problem, if not a national disgrace. For all the criticism we hear of elementary and high school instruction, what's abided at our colleges is discernibly worse.

"We don't feel the professors are here for us," we were told by a Harvard junior. "When we come to Harvard, we have to

understand it's not for the education we get, but for the reputation its degree gives us." Nathan Shipman's experience at Oregon State was more blatant. "You don't have teachers here," he
said. "I've had professors on the first day say, 'I'm here to do
research; I'm forced to teach; so you're not going to have a good
term.'" At both schools, it became clear to us that large segments of their faculties don't care about undergraduates, nor do
they feel they have to.

Harvard boasts a ratio of one professor for every seven of its
students. At least that's the figure it gives to guides like *Peterson's*
and *Barron's*. And yes, it has seminar-size courses. A senior also
noted that "even in the smallest of classes, the seminars I've taken,
like tutorials, there would be ten or twenty kids, often the professors don't even grade the papers." He recalled small classes in
Harvard's well-regarded history department "where there was a
professor who ran the class with a teaching fellow who graded the
papers. I assumed, I hoped, that the professor read the papers at
the end of the year, but it was the teaching fellow." We weren't sure
we had heard him right. *Paper readers for twenty or fewer students?*

But we had. "The same is true in all the history department
tutorials I've taken," he added.

Did the professors feel too lofty to read what their students
had written? Or were professors at both Oregon and Harvard
simply full of a quiet contempt for the undergraduates they are
ostensibly paid to teach?

A key reason that students are given short shrift is a rather
simple one. It's that research and publication have first priority:
these pave the road to promotions and outside offers. Harvard's
professors are expected to be leaders in their fields; that's why
they're there. Most of the aforesaid $125,684 budgeted per stu-
dent actually goes to them: for research assistance, sabbaticals, and
loads so light that much of their pay is for not teaching. If students
want Harvard's reputation to rub off on them, their tuitions are
paying for that burnishing.

The story is a bit different at Oregon State. It stands second in its state's system, discernibly below the flagship University of Oregon in Eugene. In this, it has many soul sisters: Iowa State, Georgia State, Michigan State. In the past, they may have accepted their subordinate status. But no longer. All of them now want to reach parity with their state's flagship. Hence the message to their faculties: Research! Write! Publish! That's how a school gets on the map. Oregon State's undergraduates feel the effects, since its professors know they will not be faulted for indifferent teaching. (At one research university we heard about, not OSU, when a group of students confronted the chair of their department about what they felt was lackluster teaching, he told them, "If you want that sort of thing you should have gone to a liberal arts school. That's not what we do here.")

At Oregon State, very few of the students we met had ever been in a professor's office to discuss materials from a class. At Harvard, things weren't much different. A student told us, "I think part of it is certainly that it's intimidating for people to go and speak to professors whom they've never really met." He then added, "I also think that a lot of people feel that they must have something really meaningful to say to a professor; that if you walk into that professor's office hours and disturb him or her you really have to have something insightful, something that will make the professor think that it was worth their while that you came by."

Here's our basic premise: every student has a mind and is curious about the wider world. The same sophomore who is now basically majoring in beer could be presenting a seminar paper on Molière's *La Malade Imaginaire*. We present this as a self-evident truth, not a speculation or surmise. Moreover, the subjects being taught are only means to an end. The mental stimulation we've cited can happen in classes in chemistry and calculus, literature and linguistics, economics or earth science. Sadly, far too few students are being encouraged to discover and develop their talents. In theory, that's why we have teachers: to stir intellects and imaginations, to open students to universes they had never known before.

In practice, this does happen; and we'll be showing how and where. But not nearly to the degree our young people desire and deserve.

Happily, the news from Cambridge isn't all disappointing. Some professors become legends. Michael Sandel's course on "Justice" packs 800 students into Harvard's Sanders Theater every fall. Of course, he lectures. Yet despite the sea of faces, he constantly throws out questions, listens closely to the responses, remarks on their implications, and often asks for a follow-up. True, these aren't the sustained interchanges one has in a small seminar. But it works. Almost all of the 800 cite Sandel as having touched them personally. He is a virtuoso teacher, able to entrance a crowded room.

"Above all," Sandel says, teaching "is about commanding attention and holding it." A large part of the skill is, at one and the same time, to give everyone something to ponder, whether they are honors majors or have come over from engineering to give the course a try.

It's a rare talent, partly cultivated, and to some degree innate. Many of the best teachers are offbeat, quirky, in fact unlike anyone their students have ever seen. One was Allan Bloom, who mesmerized a generation at Cornell as he paced puffing a Gauloise, holding forth on the politics in *Madame Bovary*. Or Michael Harrington, who wore his socialism on his sleeve, teaching a course in "Power in America" at New York's Queens College. And Conor Cruise O'Brien, at NYU in an earlier incarnation in the 1960s. He'd been a practicing politician and diplomat but was always an intellectual. (He had a lot to do with one of your authors becoming a writer.)

All had enough confidence in their own ideas to say what they believed, not what an academic discipline demanded. Incredible, passionate, awesome teachers take the whole world as their oyster bed, even if their assertions aren't always backed by formulas or footnotes. Needless to say, there's a risk of ego trips, as well as misusing classrooms for a rostrum. But students can detect that. Our point is that memorable minds are integral to education, and shouldn't be confined. The issue is not just academic freedom but introducing students to spirits who will make a difference in their lives.

Every campus has such teachers. Student evaluations at two very different schools, Oklahoma State University in Stillwater and Pomona College in California, help illustrate the point. In the more than one thousand comments we scanned, most of the professors were described as good or average or awful, with a depressing number in the final category. Still, we pressed on. Here were some diamonds we found: "An incredible professor!" "This man is a genius!" "I learned a lot just from his character." "Really makes you think about life and morality." "Open-minded, interesting, and passionate." "His zeal for the subject radiates through the room." "I know I am changed forever." "Awesome, a force of nature!" "He single-handedly changed me from being a chemistry hater to a chemistry lover."

What these assessments tell us is that great teaching comes not just from a handful of fabled professors, but often from men and women whose names aren't known beyond the campus gate. We'd like to hope that every undergraduate will have such an experience—it may be what they remember most about their college education.

Now from great to good. *Good* teaching calls for skill at *explaining*. It's an ability to clarify obscure issues or events. Like why the Battle of Gettysburg was so decisive in the Civil War, or how genetic mutations complement Darwin's original theory. Coherent organization is obviously important. But even more is sensing if students are grasping the analysis. "I watch the eyes of my students," John Lachs, a Vanderbilt philosophy teacher, told us. "When they begin to glaze over, it's a signal I am boring them." We were struck by how many professors we watched didn't scan the room that way. A furrowed brow, a raised eyebrow, a hand half-raised, all are reactions that could be followed up.

We've also observed how teachers who are adept at explaining have a store of examples, anecdotes, and, yes, jokes, to help decode abstract arguments and make abstruse ideas concrete. We acknowledge that good explaining isn't easy. But this is what professors are paid to do; if they aren't doing it competently, they should be made to find out how. "You can tell they are geniuses in their field," Patricia Albom, a sophomore at Oregon State, told us. "But some of them don't know how to teach at all."

Sad to say, a common recourse of inept instructors is to fault their pupils as indolent or inattentive. Instead, we wish they would ask themselves, how come students put in work for other professors, but not for me? Or admit, as Vanderbilt's John Lachs does, "When my teaching fails, it is because of something I have failed to do."

A second requisite is *caring*, which can be revealed in many ways and is always apparent to students. We liked how Charlene Shovic at Arizona State University expressed it. "When I can say I learned something from a class, it was because the professor was saying, 'Hey, I really want to be here for you guys.'" Another Arizona State student recalled how, by the second day of class, the professor knew everybody's name and major. "I don't know how he did it, but he did."

Daniel Bao, at Oregon State, raised a question after class, but the professor told him he didn't have the answer. "What happened afterward was he had taken the effort to find my email address and sent me the answer," Bao told us. "I was really amazed." But this experience was so exceptional that the student wanted to tell us about it.

Good teaching is only possible if professors are also active in research. We must have heard this mantra, or variants of it, from at least a dozen deans and department chairs. Active researchers, we were told, have to keep abreast of what's happening in their field, since their own studies must take account of those developments. So the courses they teach reflect the most recent thinking and findings. Conversely, professors who don't do research can be using material that is irrelevant or out of date. To this, a provost added, "You can't possibly be a good teacher unless you're interested in sharing what you've learned, both through research and publication."

All universities, and increasing numbers of colleges, now expect their faculties to discover and create new knowledge, and record it in published form. Research is the first test for preferment and promotions. Teaching reputations, by contrast, don't travel, while research and publication do. Imagine if a Stanford or a Yale hiring committee were told about an Oklahoma State professor who mesmerizes freshmen in introductory chemistry. Do you think they'd express interest in her? More likely, their first question would be: What about her publications? So research becomes the priority, with additional arguments mustered to support it. Hence the abovementioned incantation: the more we stress research, the better our teaching will be.

There's only one problem. Or rather two. First, factually, it's wrong. And second, its consequences are pernicious. In our observation, even committed undergraduates aren't asking for what's in the latest scholarly journals. Yet what scholar-professors want to teach is their research sub-specialty, or as William Bennett pointed out, "Too many faculty members want to teach their dissertation or their next article."

The table on page 84 lists some of the topics that professors choose. They are so specialized, when not esoteric, that course offerings proliferate, thwarting a broad understanding of ourselves and the world. This also explains why Stanford's history department offers no fewer than 229 separate courses. These courses weren't devised for their students. Rather, they make life easier for the professor who often just has to use notes from his last article or the galleys of her next book. So one may offer a class in Tobacco

THE NEW LIBERAL ARTS?

A Sampling of Undergraduate Courses

Quest, Riddle, and Resolution in Modernism. The secular modernist masterpiece's paradoxical attraction to mystery and transcendent experience in the context of modernism's obsession with puzzles, riddles, and quests for their solutions. (Stanford)

Realisms and Anti-Realisms. Common deployment of realism, and terms such as "reality," "reflection," "imitation," "representation," "totality," "particularity," "contingency," and "mimesis." (Stanford)

Language, Disability, Fiction. Portrayals of cognitive and linguistic impairment in modern fiction. We will examine how these characters serve as figures of otherness, transcendence, physicality, or abjection. How this abstract alternity stands in relation to contemporaneous discourses of science, sociology, ethics, politics, and aesthetics. (Yale)

Transgression and Redemption. Nathaniel Hawthorne's *The Scarlet Letter*, a Romantic novella featuring a diva-class sexual adventuress whose notorious act of transgressive love is at once reproductive and redemptive; a false buddy team of village divine and his pagan avenger locked in a tangle of stalking, persecution, and self-flagellation; and the projected specter of a Protestant Godhead so intent on punishment that the only ideas of "confession" he will abide are communal humiliation and abjection. (Duke)

and Health in World History, another on Gay Autobiography, while a colleague dilates on The Creation and Destruction of Yugoslavia. However these topics are arrived upon, a cafeteria with 229 dishwashers subverts the liberal education they came for and becomes the price students pay for choosing a college where research comes first.

Even small independent colleges, ostensibly committed to liberal arts teaching, expect their professors to conduct research. At

Williams, members of the faculty receive fully paid leaves from the classroom. When their faculty is creating knowledge about Kingship and Conflict under Louis the German, 817–876 or The Statistical Distribution of Zeros of Random Paraorthogonal Polynomials in the Unit Circle—to cite two projects highlighted on the college website—we wonder how this contributes to the education of Williams undergraduates. Of course, this is knowledge: it is knowledge that professors create for other professors. We can't say whether the faculty members did this work while on sabbatical; but we don't think that Williams students or their parents should be financing it. Yet, as Harvard's Harvey Mansfield has noted, the professors come to believe "that what they're doing research on is exactly what students need to know." But since Williams doesn't have graduate students, they inflict their microspecialties on near-at-hand undergraduates.

Unfortunately, the push for more research seems to be only intensifying. When we began working on this book we attended the 2007 meeting of the American Sociological Association. Between sessions, we counted up the number of papers listed in the program. They totaled 3,015—an all-time high, we later learned. A little research, if you'll forgive the term, revealed that in 1985 only 502 papers were presented, and the number of sociologists barely grew. Of course, sociology is just one case. But if it's typical of the thirty or so fields that make up the liberal arts, it means some 90,000 papers are prepared each year. Nor have we included vocational subjects like aeronautical engineering and sports management, all of which have their conferences and journals.

Is all this research truly necessary? We suppose we're obliged to aver that we fully support the expansion and enrichment of knowledge. Given the attributes bestowed on us by our evolution, we have a duty to advance our understanding of ourselves and the world we share. So how can we appear to oppose research? After all, that would appear to be our view, since we seem to be suggesting that few of those 3,015 sociological papers needed to be written.

Here's why: most of what is now being done under the guise of academic research isn't really that. Of course, each of these projects adds something to our knowledge. We now know more about some aspects of women's hockey and middle-aged policemen, two of the sociologists' offerings. Are we suggesting that these are things we don't need to know? Part of us says yes—the world would remain just as enlightened had these topics remained unexplored. But as we have noted, our recurring argument is that the time and energy and resources spent on all these papers and articles and books can and should be devoted to better classroom teaching.

The pressure to publish can also be counterproductive. We learned this from Douglas Smith, a Montana biologist, who helped to reintroduce gray wolves into Yellowstone National Park. He told us that when he's searching the behavior of carnivores, the research has frequently been sliced and diced into so many publications (so that authors can take credit for multiple articles) that it's hard to figure out what it all means. "It frustrates me because the authors take a study and split it into three or four publications," Smith told us. "So the whole story isn't even in that journal. It might be in two or three different places, and I have to search them out myself."

Douglas Smith probably knows more about gray wolves than anyone on our planet. But academic biologists don't give him a high rating because he only writes when he believes it's necessary. "In scientific circles, I'm judged by the length of my publication list," he said. "That's always the first question."

We're disheartened by efforts at liberal arts colleges to transform themselves into mini-research universities. It's not their role, nor is it something they do well. At Williams College, in a recent year, its website listed 133 publications or conference papers by members of its faculty. A new mantra of college presidents is that if they do not underwrite this research, their professors will leave for larger schools that do. That's one more myth. Those who do get bids from the major leagues almost invariably pack and go. But the truth is that few receive such invitations, which leads us to think that minor league research isn't important enough to interest the leading institutions.

Nor are four-year arts colleges the only institutions afflicted by the publishing virus. The virus has spread to the community colleges, nursing schools, and lower-tier colleges that previously functioned well without having their professors' names in journals. Claudia periodically gets calls from junior professors at such schools asking for her view on how, say, new technologies impact news gathering and reporting. What emerges is that the callers need fodder for a "paper" to be presented at a professional conference. It's all just compost to bulk up résumés. At higher levels, the touchstone is how often you are cited by your colleagues. There are even databases showing the number of times each professor has been mentioned in other people's footnotes.

We're even uneasy about such research at a Harvard or a Berkeley, since it subverts the quality and content of undergraduate courses and majors—and it changes the school's priorities. This can best be seen in the current economic crisis besetting the University of California system. Its president, Mark Yudof, sent pink slips to the adjuncts teaching basic undergraduate courses like composition and mathematics, while all the senior faculty had to absorb were a few days of furloughs. Yudof's main plaint was that budget cuts might cause the system to lose its most visible stars. His mission—as an heir to Clark Kerr—seems to be to shed popular education and become a chain of research institutes.

Is there anything wrong with teachers teaching what they know? After all, neurologists base how they treat their patients on what practitioners in their specialty take to be understood. The same holds for firefighters and four-star chefs. But a difference is that professors are also given the responsibility of teaching liberal arts, and for that, their audience consists of undergraduates. And what professors know—their *academic knowledge*—can become not only an impediment but actually undermine the very aims of liberal education. Do we really want, as Charles Maier, an exceptional Harvard historian, has said of his colleagues, undergraduate teaching that "essentially says students should understand how scholars do scholarship"?

If medieval sages hoped to discover a Philosopher's Stone, their modern counterparts seek to propound theories. This has always been the quest in science: who will be the next Newton, Einstein,

---

THREE SIMPLE SUGGESTIONS

Monitor Laptops. When visiting classes, we often sat in the back of the room. As a result, we could observe something not seen by the instructor: how laptops were being used by the students who brought them. In almost all the classes we attended, at least half the screens displayed games of solitaire, reruns of sporting events, messages to friends. In pre-laptop days, students might daydream—but at least the instructor was the center of attention.

Stop PowerPointing. If using PowerPoint continues, students will spend their entire college career in darkened rooms where their instructors cannot even see their expressions. Files of slides etch the day's outline in stone; new ideas can't be added, as they can on a chalkboard. If graphs or pictures are needed, they should be photocopied beforehand and handed out as the class starts.

Preventing Plagiarism. Plagiarism is as much the fault of lazy instructors as it is of dilatory students. Assigning generic topics, like *The Heart of Darkness* or the Congress of Vienna, makes it too easy to copy from fraternity files or purchase papers from an internet service. Instructors should make clear that all papers must allude to discussions and reading in this semester's class.

Darwin? Today professors of philosophy hope to emulate Thomas Kuhn's *paradigm shifts*. For psychologists, the goal is to create a rubric akin to Leon Festinger's *cognitive dissonance*. Sociologists would retire happy for being associated with a phrase like Robert Merton's *self-fulfilling prophecy*. Today's most apposite model may be Judith Butler, of the University of California at Berkeley, who is widely cited for coining *regulative discourse, performativity*, and *frameworks of intelligibility*. If you are languishing at Central Missouri State and yearn for a call to a higher tier, the way out and up is to become linked with a locution that sounds abstract and analytical, and then hope it wends its way into professorial parlance.

The shift toward theory, or what passes for it, began in the 1960s as part of academe's revolt against anything established. While the Vietnam War and the Selma-Montgomery march saw shedding of real blood, the coming cohort of tenured faculty embraced *stochastic models* and *performativity texts*. But instead of attacking the liberal arts as a bourgeois diversion, as a previous generation did, an easier route was to retain that label but decant the contents. Out went Aristotle and in his stead came Althusser, while Dickens was replaced by Derrida and Locke by Lacan. Many sincerely believed that subjecting texts to deconstruction would undermine the foundations of corporate capitalism. But for teaching undergraduates, the quest for theory is not only misdirected, it warps the whole ambience of education.

If anything, there's an inverse correlation between good teaching and academic research. We saw how the students at Oregon State felt shortchanged by their classes, because even their second-tier school was pushing the faculty to put publishing first. In 2008 and 2009 the National Survey of Student Engagement asked undergraduates at various colleges to rate their professors on "helpfulness" and "availability." This seems to us a good gauge of how they felt about the education they were getting. The scores ran from a high of just over 80 to a low a bit below 40. Uniformly, the most satisfied students were at smaller schools, not always well known: Centre College in Kentucky (81); Earlham in Indiana (78); Augsburg in Minnesota (77); and Hendrix in Arkansas (75).

Professors at large state universities whose faculties are urged to pursue research scored notably lower: University of North Carolina (48); University of Virginia (46); University of Iowa (45); University of Michigan (40); and University of Minnesota (39). Nor is the satisfaction gap surprising. Classes at Earlham and Augsburg are more likely to have 25 students. At North Carolina and Iowa, 250 is a more common figure.

Potsdam College, in Upstate New York, believes their pioneering program in undergraduate mathematics works precisely because they do *not* try to link teaching and research. Their statement:

> The two primary activities for a professor are teaching and scholarship or research. It is generally presumed that these two activities serve to reinforce one another. In mathematics, rather, they tend to adversely affect one another. The information with which a mathematics research project deals is usually inaccessible to undergraduates.

The same could be said for the sciences. Properly taught and understood, the sciences are part of the liberal arts. Indeed, from Aristotle's time until the modern era, the sciences were called *Natural Philosophy*, affirming their affinity with the totality of knowledge. We would like to think that professors of biology and chemistry still take out time to muse about the order—or chaos—of the natural world. Even more, we want to believe that they could teach—or join in teaching—introductory courses that would present the hopes of their chosen field and the goals of science as a whole. But such classes are exceedingly rare, even at a time when we are warned that lay citizens are woefully uninformed about science. When colleges impose a science requirement, it can usually be fulfilled by taking, say, the traditional Chemistry 101, which is simply that department's entry course and makes no effort to be a broad survey of what science is and does.

Nor have the humanities been immune. It even seeps down to freshmen classes. We came across a syllabus for a composition course at a public college. The reading assignments for the last three weeks consisted of essays titled "Right of Death and Power Over Life," "Docile Bodies," and "The Body of the Condemned"— all by Michel Foucault, a notoriously abstruse French philosopher. We want young people to have guidance in writing clearly and coherently. Are they being taught Foucault in order to achieve this goal? Or are they being laden with esoteric texts because instructors in English 101 tend to be PhD candidates and so are beholden to their postgraduate mentors?

To de-link teaching and research is not to offer students the easy route. Good teaching doesn't require—indeed, doesn't tolerate—spoon-feeding or dumbing down. On the contrary, good teaching sets high expectations and warns that serious learning will be difficult. Indeed, it places students at center stage; they are the ones to be persuaded to use their minds. And in this pursuit, less is often more. It is common to hear professors boasting of assigning several hundred pages of reading a week. There's no way that much material can be absorbed in seven days. More will be retained from two carefully chosen articles.

This unconcern for students inflicts a lot of human damage. David Harris of the University of Southern Maine admits that in his course on human anatomy and physiology, "the amount of material is overwhelming." And it is the main reason why 20 percent of his students regularly fail. But is the problem here the students or the professor? Even in anatomy and physiology, there are topics that could be abbreviated without the sky falling. A one-in-five failure rate should be unacceptable.

Carol Twigg, who heads the National Center for Academic Transformation, has studied hundreds of colleges. She told us that drops, failures, or withdrawals of up to 45 percent are not unusual in freshmen courses. To her mind, it goes far toward telling us why so many don't make it to their sophomore year. The greatest single scandal in American higher education is what happens— and doesn't happen—in the first semester. Though no one has collated full figures, we estimate that over a quarter, more likely at least a third, of all freshmen fail to return. Just to cite one state, at three of Missouri's state campuses, non-return rates for freshmen are 35 percent, 36 percent, and 44 percent. True, some choose to transfer or continue with college later. But most won't. What is happening in Missouri isn't out of the ordinary.

It's not frequent that a college openly admits it has a teaching problem. But Harvard did. Perhaps it had read the Princeton Review's survey of its students, who gave their professors C– on their classroom performance, and D for their outside-of-class avail- ability, the lowest grades in the Golden Dozen. Hence it appointed a "task force"—which sounds more engaged than a committee—to find out what had gone wrong and suggest remedies. All but one of its members held endowed chairs (the William Maier Professor of Political Economy, the Sosland Family Professor of Romance Lan- guages and Literatures). No junior faculty, no teaching assistants, and notably no students were invited to serve.

Still, the panel began by hearing testimony from some under- graduates. They complained that all too "many faculty are not really interested in them." The students' response was a "take a passive stance toward the classroom and turn their passions into extracurricular activities." Apparently these grievances hit home. The task force was forced to conclude that though Harvard had some "creative and devoted teachers," upward of half their col- leagues might not deserve that designation. In our view, this was the high point of their eighty-three-page report titled "A Compact to Enhance Teaching and Learning at Harvard." So the challenge was how to get underperforming professors to change their ways.

We found the report's proposals as revealing as the findings. Here are three that caught our eyes.

The first suggested that "rewards"—later specified as "salary improvements"—be proffered to professors who agreed to take some time from their research and devote it to their classrooms. The premise, of course, is that Harvard faculty cannot be *told* what to do, say, like reading and grading students' papers, not to mention teaching a section of an introductory course. The only open option, it appears, is financial inducement on a campus where full professors already average $192,600 a year.

The next suggestion was to set up "a system in which faculty colleagues visit one another's classes to learn and comment." Our response was to wonder why a *system* is needed for something so simple and sensible. Indeed, if professors haven't done this themselves, we wonder how concerned they are about their teaching. At smaller colleges, we saw instructors paying mutual visits without formalities. And it helps. We were present when one asked a colleague why he hadn't called on a certain student. "She didn't raise her hand," he was told. "But didn't you notice her puzzled expression when you were on Canto XII of the *Inferno*?"

Their third suggestion was more concrete: "All junior faculty should be urged to do individual videotape sessions." That sounds innovative and up to date. It's increasingly common to have tapes or films made so teachers can see themselves in action. Some are shocked; others admit nothing untoward. (It's really necessary, albeit more expensive, to have several cameras so some can catch the students' expressions.) What struck us was that at Harvard it was only the *junior faculty* who were to be urged to be recorded. Yet at Harvard and elsewhere we heard that some of the best teaching was, as one student put it, by younger staff who are "more energetic and interested in interacting with students." In fact, complaints about senior faculty were more frequent and widespread. Even so, the task force chose to spare Harvard's 839 full professors from possible taping, reserving it for its 372 instructors and assistant professors. (We're not sure where the 170 associate professors fit.) This seems to confess that there is no way to induce the tenured faculty to accept professional improvement. But to exempt them from even an invitation list said to us that the task force put the sensibilities of their middle-aged colleagues before their own students' desire for better teaching.

There's a more troubling question about teaching undergraduates that wasn't raised or answered. The task force's implicit premise was that Harvard's professors could do a better classroom job if they weren't under such pressure to publish. So if they had some of that burden lifted, they would be able to apply themselves and present stimulating courses. Thus the reasoning ran that the pedagogical potential is there. We wish we could be that sure. It's possible that the problem is not one of time, but of competence. Some faculty just lack the constitution to relate effectively to young people. After all, not everyone has aptitudes for everything. Still, we'll grant there are professors who, were they willing to be mentored, might raise their teaching level from, say, a C to a middling B.

But the real question here has to do with the faculty's commitment to change. When a faculty meeting was convened at Harvard to discuss the "Compact," Eric Mazur, a physics professor we know who had been a member of the task force, told us it had the lowest turnout he could recall. "They didn't see this report as something that will affect them; if they did, they would have shown up." A report on revising campus parking rules, he hazarded, would have filled more seats.

· 6 ·

THE TRIUMPH OF TRAINING

The very phrase *liberal arts* induces hushed respect. In an era when bachelor's degrees are awarded in sports management and fashion merchandising, hearing of students who are majoring in philosophy and history still evokes our esteem. The liberal arts may be viewed as a classical education and an intellectual adventure, as learning for its own sake and pursuing the life of the mind. The most admired purlieus of higher education are its liberal arts colleges, which generally enroll only undergraduates and eschew vocational programs.

Almost all universities have liberal arts divisions (sometimes "arts and sciences," occasionally "arts and letters") although they vary in quality and status. At Princeton and Stanford, they are regarded as the preeminent undergraduate program. Although liberal learning is respected on flagship campuses such as Ann Arbor, Madison, and Chapel Hill, graduate programs absorb a greater share of resources and command more faculty attention. Other state schools, like Texas A&M or Purdue, have liberal arts divisions. But much of their time and teaching goes to bread-and-butter courses for students in vocational programs. MIT has some liberal arts departments and even offers a few majors, but they are mainly taken by students who found that science and engineering wasn't their thing. Cal Tech also has some liberal arts professors; however, it isn't possible to major in their fields. At best, you can set up a double major with a science degree. What this brief review really tells us is that except at independent colleges, the liberal arts have a peripheral place in most of American higher education.

On first encounter, the fields of study that make up the liberal arts look much as they've always been. College catalogs still list departments named philosophy, anthropology, or chemistry. But a closer look at offerings in, say, psychology or literature will find that though the bottles have the same labels, what's inside is markedly different. Of course, there's nothing wrong with adjusting to changing times. That's why we now sometimes see "earth sciences" instead of geology, and why at least one school has replaced psychology with "psychological and brain sciences." We now acknowledge that to understand our personalities and our planet depends on many disciplines. But our concern in this chapter is not with the complexity of modern knowledge. Rather, our interest is with what has happened to the liberal arts. And that in turn calls for examining how its undergraduate courses are currently designed and taught.

As discussed in the previous chapters, courses meant to prove one's fealty to a specialized discipline seem to us a road utterly mistaken. There are other constrictions in the curriculum, however, that are also of great concern. The first is a kind of narrowing of vision by those committed to teaching the liberal arts. The second is the encroachment of training upon learning.

At one time, the centerpiece of the liberal arts consisted of college-wide courses, designed to impart what an educated person ought to know. These classes weren't "interdisciplinary," even when taught by professors from varied fields. They could more appropriately be called supra-disciplinary, since they weren't constricted by the content and methods of specific subjects. At Columbia, one sequence was called *Contemporary Civilization*, wherein faculty from all over the campus participated. Thus someone from economics could lead a discussion on *Macbeth*, just as a colleague from psychology could explain the Treaty of Versailles. This approach to the liberal arts saw it as being taught and studied by serious laypeople, unimpeded by the apparatus of professional specialties. To the credit of Columbia, this class is still on the books. However, what's changed is that far fewer senior professors deign to take part, so the bulk of the teaching is given over to adjuncts and graduate assistants.

Amherst College had its *Evolution of the Earth and Man*, which professors of astronomy, geology, and biology created. They not only sat in on one another's lectures, but led all the discussion sections. While they had been trained in particular fields, they too were willing and able to grasp and teach ideas that make for a common scientific culture. The course has long departed. We were told that the current faculty have more specialized career goals.

Perhaps pride of place goes to the University of Chicago. To show its concern for undergraduates, they were given their own faculty who were not immersed in postgraduate teaching. We talked with one of its products, Frank Wilzcek, a winner of the Nobel Prize in physics and now an MIT professor. He had grown up in a New York City outer borough, a child genius in an unlikely setting. "The University of Chicago really woke me up," he told us. "I remember an extraordinary literature class. We did this close reading of *Paradise Lost*, and you realized the structures really hang together. It's like music, where themes recur." We asked if that might have helped him on the path that led to the Nobel. He smiled.

In living memory, there were professors like David Riesman, C. Wright Mills, and Margaret Mead, who spoke and wrote directly for a thoughtful public. The same held for John Kenneth Galbraith as an economist, along with Carl Sagan and Jacob Bronowski in the sciences. Nor did these scholars wear two hats. They conversed the same way with their students and colleagues as they did with their larger audience. More than that, they felt passionately about the realms they explored, showing that minds can be enlarged and invigorated by a sense of purpose. But this link between professors and public has been severed, largely due to the constraints imposed by academic disciplines, indeed the divorce of academic knowledge from everyday understanding. What distresses us as much as anything is that young professors who might be a Mills, a Mead, or a Bronowski fear they will be dismissed as popularizers by senior colleagues who hold sway over their careers.

The liberal arts are defined by the scope of their vision, and that breadth should be celebrated, not artificially limited. Of equal, if not greater, concern for us, however, is the potential displacement of that vision entirely.

So let's pay a visit to New Mexico State University, a thriving public institution in Las Cruces, some forty miles from El Paso. In Breland Hall, you'll find students majoring in philosophy, immersed in classes in *Epistemology, Formal Logic,* and *Philosophy of Mind.* To our thinking, this is the heart of higher education, and it can be pursued in Las Cruces, New Mexico, as well as Cambridge, Massachusetts.

Over in Thomas Hall on the same campus, you'll meet undergraduates who have chosen hotel, motel, and resort management. Their classes include *Quantity Food Production, Gaming Operations,* and *Beverage Management,* for which they will receive a bachelor's degree. If epistemology ranks as higher education, our view is beverage management does not.

It isn't education. It is training. At best, it should be a sequence in a community college or in a professional program at the post-graduate level. Nor is beverage management an exotic example.

Most campuses now devote more resources to vocational concentrations, since their majors now outnumber those in liberal arts fields. In 2008, the most recent figures as we write, degrees in the "hospitality" sphere surpassed those awarded in philosophy.

In fact, vocational training has long been entrenched in America's colleges. Even now, more students at MIT major in engineering than the sciences. The Ivy League's University of Pennsylvania welcomes undergraduates to its business school, and it is their most popular choice (and we'll be saying more about it). The federal government sponsors four vocational academies to serve as grooming grounds for future officers.

So there wasn't a Golden Age when everyone chose fields like history and literature, or for that matter, astronomy and physics. On the contrary, for many years, preparing schoolteachers topped the list. Still, until the mid-1960s, there was essentially an even balance between vocational training and the liberal arts. Even if some students would go on to law or medicine, they weren't preoccupied by those professions from their freshman year. As our table on page 100 of the top ten majors shows, business programs have made the most striking gains since 1968, followed by health fields. Psychology is the only traditional liberal arts field that has grown in popularity, perhaps due to our nation's preoccupation with the self. So have the fine and performing arts, now bolstered by cinema studies and video production. The growth in the "other" category results from the rise of new applied majors like fashion merchandising, sports management, and crime scene investigation.

The biggest losers have been the social sciences, humanities, and the physical sciences. English now attracts only half the majors it did in the mid-1960s, while history and foreign languages and literature have even fewer survivors. Physical science majors are down by 60 percent. And relative to total enrollments only a quarter as many students are choosing mathematics. As a result, in once esteemed fields fewer professors are being hired and those who

THE TOP TEN MAJORS

Per 1,000 Bachelor's Degrees Awarded

1968		2008	
Education	213	Business	215
Social Sciences	191	Social Sciences	108
Business	128	Humanities	86
Humanities	115	Education	69
Physical Sciences	68	Health	67
Engineering	59	Psychology	59
Biology	50	Fine Arts	56
Fine Arts	40	Engineering	54
Psychology	38	Communications	51
Health	28	Biology	49
Other Vocational	70	Other Vocational	186
	1,000		1,000
All Vocational	498	All Vocational	642

NOTE: Social Sciences include History; Physical Sciences include Mathematics; Fine Arts include Performing Arts.

retire are unlikely to be replaced. Some departments have been abolished, while others are swept under generic programs. At George Mason University, you can no longer major in French and German, or Latin or Greek. As it happens, mathematics departments continue to prosper, but it's due to college-wide requirements that fill their freshman sections. But most of those students are there under duress, and at best 1 percent who begin end up making mathematics their major.

Since 1960, the proportion of young Americans attending college has essentially doubled. This expansion has meant that more students would be the first in their families to enroll. It's not surprising that many of them would pick vocational majors. After all, the stay-in-school message they've heard is that a degree brings higher earnings and status. When we visited Oregon State University, we talked with some students from such backgrounds who had chosen to study liberal arts subjects. They told us they were constantly badgered by parents and relatives who wanted to know how supposedly useless subjects would help them move up the social ladder. It isn't easy for freshmen to frame responses to such concerns.

Our argument for ending vocational training has several strands. To start, we deem it a huge mistake to squander years that could and should be devoted to enriching young minds. This is what the best colleges now endeavor to do. (But not always: the ten universities in our Golden Dozen all offer engineering degrees.) To devote that irreplaceable period in one's life to ornamental horticulture or pastry arts subverts a sensible purview of higher education. But we also have practical objections. One is that vocational programs are chosen while students are applying from high school. While most seventeen-year-olds are natively bright and able to learn, there's one thing they don't know, and there is no way they can at their age. It is what the world of adult careers is actually like.

Even if a parent is, say, an accountant or a sports announcer, teenagers can't have more than a cursory grasp of what they do while at work. We'd even hazard that twenty-one or twenty-two, the usual ages of college graduation, may be too early to decide that dentistry or resort management is the career for you. The best thing after receiving a bachelor's degree may be to find a semi-skilled job—Best Buy or Old Navy?—and keep your eyes and

mind open about career choices. The Department of Labor currently lists 1,400 different occupations, from aerobics to zoologists. Right now, new ones are being created, and many don't yet
have names.

As we've noted, business has become the most popular undergraduate major. Regardless of our own opinions about whether it
rates as *higher* or even as *education*, it has gained a prominent
place on our campuses, not least by displacing less practical
majors. So we feel obliged to take a look at what is being taught
and learned in its classes. Penn's Wharton School intrigues us, if
only because it is regularly rated as the top undergraduate business program. It certainly takes itself seriously. Its freshmen, just a
summer away from high school, are solemnly informed that they
will be inculcated in "innovation, leadership, global perspectives,
and managing change." So let's review *Management 100*, which
all students must take in their first semester. An aim of the course
is to teach them to be team players, a trait presumably expected in
executive circles. Large lecture sections are broken into groups of
ten, each of which is given an off-campus assignment. One recent
task called for organizing an event at a nearby jazz club to raise
awareness for World AIDS Day. Another was to design a fire safety
program for a local elementary school. (While this goes on, other
Penn freshmen are pondering Herodotus and Galileo.) Each group
has a *team advisor*, to provide guidance and lead discussion
sections.

We were bemused to learn that these mentors are not members
of the faculty, or even graduate students. Rather, they are other
undergraduates who had taken the course earlier. We grant the
importance of learning to work in teams, and good teachers often
set groups of students to work on their own. Our problem with
Wharton's method is that few sophomores have the fund of information, techniques for coping with questions, or the skills for conducting discussions that college-level teaching requires.

For a further perspective on business training, we decided to visit classes at a less selective institution, as it would be more in line with most colleges throughout the country. We did this at Florida Gulf Coast University, a regional campus that takes 76 percent of its applicants. One class we observed was called *Global Marketing* and was taught by Ludmilla Wells, an associate professor who has a PhD in business from the University of Tennessee. Her own business experience, she told us, had been with a small advertising agency in New Jersey quite some time ago. Another course dealt with *Market Strategy*, taught by an energetic young man named Khaled Aboulnasr, who held a business doctorate from the University of Houston. His career has been entirely academic, and so he never worked in a profit-seeking enterprise. We learned this is common: business schools prefer professors with PhDs to men and women who have had hands-on careers. Indeed, accreditation expects that a majority of regular faculty have doctoral degrees.

The students we joined were all undergraduates, mainly juniors, aged about nineteen or twenty. Professor Aboulnasr's PowerPoints began with five "growth strategies": line extension, brand extension, new brands, flanking brands, and fighting brands. All were accompanied by brief examples. So when Coca-Cola bought Minute Maid, it didn't change the name to Cola-Maid. Then came three guidelines for introducing new products: consistency, resources, and demand. There followed four stages in the launching: originating ideas, screening ideas, business analysis, and test marketing. Concluding with the three basic aims of advertising: to inform, to persuade, to remind.

In *Global Marketing,* Professor Wells also had the lights down and her PowerPoints up for the entire hour. However, she relied less on lists than theatrical phrases: proactive stimuli, product life cycle, significant internal events, backward innovation, discretionary product adaptation, and saturated domestic markets. All these, the students dutifully transcribed in notebooks or laptops. The class was broken into smaller groups. One, which we watched, was assigned to plan a strategy for introducing a line of sunglasses into India.

In both classes, the professors kept posing questions to the class. But of thirty or so students in each, no more than a handful responded. The reason was soon apparent. These undergraduates had no experience in business apart from the case studies in their textbook, and certainly not at the executive level.

Yet this is going on in business classes throughout the country. There are two sides to the equation. On the one hand, half a million freshmen enroll in business programs each year, hoping that what they will learn will give them an extra edge in their subsequent careers. On the other hand, professors are needed if there are to be classes. But it was soon evident to us that it wasn't completely clear to either professors or students exactly what the students should be learning. Curriculums are filled with lists and locutions, along with quasi-theories from their field's academic journals. Professors ask students to play being senior management, and plan corporate strategy ranging from outsourcing sneakers to selling sunglasses.

What should business programs be doing instead? We'll start by saying that what is presented in their classes has no relation to what they'll be doing in their first job. Whether from Wharton or Gulf Coast, when undergraduates emerge with a business degree, if the Bank of America hires them, it won't seat them in boardrooms to plan global strategies. More likely, they will be sent to a Fresno suburb, where their job will be crunching numbers on mortgage applications—or at least we hope the bank is finally checking on the reliability of applicants. Then the newbie will listen while senior colleagues explain how and why they make their decisions. We'd like to think that liberal arts students can just as quickly pick up what will be expected in their first years on the job. Nor is this wishful thinking. Costco's chief executive majored in sociology, the head of Goldman Sachs was an English major, and the chairmen of IBM, Procter & Gamble, Union Pacific, and Wyeth all graduated with degrees in history.

We wish we could persuade undergraduates contemplating business majors to choose the liberal arts route. But this won't be easy so long as anxieties about the future infuse their decisions. A more effective step would be for colleges, whether freestanding or within universities, to simply state that they don't and won't offer vocational majors.

Engineering has long been an undergraduate program, indeed going back to the Morrill Act. A problem, as we've noted, is that they are predicated on having high school seniors make a career choice. A study conducted at the University of Pittsburgh found that of freshmen who embark on engineering, over half never leave with a degree. Each year, the Princeton Review asks undergraduates across the country to comment on their classes. Its 2010 edition found that the colleges most often cited for abysmal teaching were schools of engineering. Among the worst offenders were Stevens Institute, Rensselaer, Georgia Tech, Illinois Institute of Technology, along with the fabled Cal Tech with its galaxy of science stars.

In conversing with students at one of these schools—we'll forbear from saying which—we were told that their professors felt no obligation to make their courses interesting, let alone exciting. Instead, they preferred to assume that students arrived strongly committed to the engineering profession, ready to absorb whatever the faculty felt they had to know, no matter how ineptly presented. In this vein, their freshman sections were designed to "weed out" students—a recurrent phrase—rather than encourage them. This attitude is passed on to section assistants, most of whom are new to teaching and often have accents that make them barely comprehensible. Indeed, postgraduate engineering programs have to admit large numbers of foreign applicants because so few Americans survive the undergraduate ordeal. Without these overseas recruits, schools would have to stop awarding graduate degrees, which is the chief source of status for professors.

Should engineering be entirely a graduate offering? That's our feeling, since students would enter at the age of twenty-two, or even later, when they are better able to consider careers. (The top business schools, like Harvard and Stanford, want their applicants to be well into their twenties.) We may also find that an engineering degree doesn't need four or five years, especially when students are more mature. Professors like to elongate programs because it allows them to spin out their hyperspecialties. Even law schools are beginning to admit that their third year isn't necessary.

The same holds for nursing, which has long been an undergraduate major, each year awarding some 55,000 bachelor's degrees. As it happens, about the same number of nurses—57,000 in a recent year—obtain equally good training for associate degrees in hundreds of two-year colleges. In fact, both are accepted as suitable preparation for the Registered Nurse examination, which is now given nationally. The main difference is that the bachelor's degrees demand more courses in pure science, like organic chemistry, microbiology, and molecular genetics. These requirements look good on college websites, but no evidence is provided on how they connect with effective nursing. So there's something more at issue. Professors who teach vocational skills realize that insofar as what they do is viewed as practical (like how to wield a syringe or monitor ICUs), it lowers their status in their college community. So we're increasingly seeing vocational training aspiring to theoretical heights.

The University of San Diego now offers seminars in *Nursing Process Theory, Transcultural Nursing Models,* and *Humanistic Nursing Theory.* It boasts of having granted over 150 PhDs in its profession. We are asked to be pleased that hands-on training is being supplanted by transcultural models and humanistic theories. For our part, we're less than impressed. We often hear there is a shortage of nurses willing to work in hospital wards and public clinics, especially on weekends and nights. As more practitioners are told they should study more theory, we wonder who will be available for the 10 p.m. to 6 a.m. shifts.

There is much talk of "human capital," which usually translates into the level of skills possessed by a population. A common corollary is that more time spent in formal education makes people more proficient and productive. Hence the assertion that "investing" in education at every level will have a practical payoff. We wonder how far this is really true. We'll be devoting a chapter to trying to find what happens to individuals—how they change— due to time spent at college. The short answer is that no one really knows. Of course, nurses and engineers learn technical skills, many of which come from being taught how and when to use devices employed in their professions. Engineering also calls for quantitative competence, although it is less linked to academic mathematics than is often asserted. (Engineering is more about working up good estimates than being accurate to the fifth decimal place.) And truth to tell, we have yet to hear of "skills" worth calling that which are imparted in business courses. The best study we've seen was carried out by Norton Grubb of Berkeley and Marvin Lazerson at the University of Pennsylvania. They found that the most crucial skills are learned on the job, across all occupations and professions. "The abilities necessary in employment," they write, "are dependent on the work setting itself." Of course, an accounting firm wants their recruits to know the profession's standards and rules. But even more important is learning how these procedures are put to work in the Price Waterhouse Coopers milieu.

We acknowledge that going for a vocational degree offers one advantage. Suppose you have majored in fashion merchandising. The odds are that Old Navy will give your application priority over one from a classmate who has a degree in history. But it's not because they are impressed with courses you have taken in apparel design. So far as Old Navy is concerned, you'll learn their ways once they break you in at one of their stores. Rather, you'll have an extra edge because your choice of major shows a willingness to devote your college years to fashion, which in turn denotes your commitment to a career in their field. A history major might leave after a year, to go to law school.

We've met former business majors, now nearing middle age, who say they regret not having studied philosophy while at college. We have yet to meet a philosophy major who felt he or she should have chosen business.

SOME BACHELOR'S DEGREES AWARDED IN 2008

Equine science and management

Ornamental horticulture

Poultry science

Turf and grass management

Landscape architecture

Exercise physiology

E-Commerce

Tourism and travel management

Resort management

Knowledge management

Apparel and accessories marketing

Baking and pastry arts

Photojournalism

Animation technology

Computer systems security

Ceramic engineering

Robotics technology

Hazardous materials management

Diesel mechanics technology

Adult development and aging

Sign language interpretation

Medical office assisting

Cytotechnology

Music therapy

Medical illustration

Asian herbology

Systems science and theory

Historic preservation

Sport management

Welding technology

Furniture design

Commercial and advertising art

Fiber, textile and weaving arts

PART 3

SOME IMMODEST PROPOSALS

WHY COLLEGE COSTS SO MUCH

$192,520: that's the bare-bones cost for four years at Kenyon College, a well-regarded liberal arts school in rural Ohio. We cite it because its tab is fairly typical for colleges having known names. Kenyon is often the fallback choice when Jennifer or Jeremy fail to get fat envelopes from Dartmouth or Brown.

At Kenyon, in 2009, tuition and added fees came to $40,240, plus a relatively modest $7,890 for room and books and board. So Kenyon's basic total is $49,290, almost two-thirds the after-tax income of the typical household with college-age offspring. Granted, not everyone pays the full tab. But at Kenyon, over half the students or their parents write that close-to-$50,000 check. For almost all students receiving "financial aid," it is simply a discount on the tuition, not a cash grant. Altogether, 62 percent of its students have to take out loans to pursue a Kenyon degree.

Of course, public colleges cost less, as would living at home. But then Kenyon describes itself as the home of "world-class scholars teaching an outstanding student body."

And what, besides room, board, and books are students getting for the almost $200,000 price? Apparently, outstanding students and scholarship must be complemented by luxurious amenities. Kenyon recently opened a $70 million palace of a gym, complete with a twenty-lane swimming pool, indoor tennis and squash courts, an all-weather running track, Wi-Fi Internet, and two hundred pieces of exercise equipment. On deck are plans for a new dormitory complex, where students will live in duplex apartments similar in style to the affluent neighborhoods where many of them were raised.

Considering the amenities—plus the additional price of textbooks, electronics, sporting equipment, snacks in town with friends, plane tickets home during holidays—four years at Kenyon can easily cost a family a quarter of a million dollars. As the late Illinois senator Everett Dirksen used to say about government programs, "A billion here, a billion there, and we're soon talking real money."

At $40,240 for tuition, Kenyon is not unique in its pricing. The Sherman Antitrust Act aside, pretty much all the private liberal arts colleges in its class charge strikingly similar fees. For example: Reed, $39,700; Hamilton, $39,760; Carleton, $39,777; Franklin & Marshall, $39,980; Bowdoin, $40,020; Dickinson, $40,139; Hobart, $40,221; Wesleyan, $40,392.

According to the College Board, since 1982 tuition charges at private colleges have ballooned more than two and a half times in inflation-adjusted dollars. That's right. For every $1,000 parents were asked to pay in 1982, they must hand over $2,540 in real money today. At public colleges, the rise has been even greater, though their charges still average less than 30 percent of what private schools set. However, as we write, the University of California, long the best public system in the country, is about to raise its tuition by a third, while admitting fewer students and cutting instructional staff and classes.

It isn't easy to get reliable answers about why college costs as much as it does; financial officers are nothing if not creative in spreading out expenses. At many schools, few of the costs of a new stadium are charged to the football team. Or the budgets of expensive graduate programs are commingled with those of the undergraduate curriculum.

Most colleges and universities enjoy nonprofit, tax-exempt status, which makes them less subject to scrutiny than other types of enterprises. Whereas corporations are expected to report their numbers to the Securities and Exchange Commission, nonprofit colleges are far less monitored. Furthermore, a general sense of goodwill toward higher education results in its getting a pass on financial activities. The public doesn't have the same skepticism about our colleges and universities that it has about the health care system or the banks—but it should.

How exactly tuition costs are arrived at is a great mystery. Iowa's Charles Grassley, the ranking Republican on the Senate Banking Committee, has made nonprofit finances a specialty for which he has a staff of seasoned lawyers and investigators. Yet he admitted to us that he didn't know how tuition costs are set. "You'd be paying fifteen dollars for a gallon of milk if it had gone up as fast as tuition in the past twenty years; that's how out of whack it is." He went on: "When I ask public and private institutions why tuition has to go up two or three times the rate of inflation, I never really get a realistic answer."

When it comes to tuition, the schools generally claim that fees don't begin to cover their costs. In its most recent reporting, for 2008, Williams said it spent $70,316 on each of its students. While its sticker tuition then was $37,640, it collected an average of $23,468, so $46,848 had to come from other sources. But we want to ask: why $70,316? For a contrast, we visited Linfield College, in Oregon's wine country, where we found an excellent liberal arts education was offered for $26,603. They took in $20,334 per student, leaving only a $6,269 gap. We would argue that Williams could do just as well by its students on Linfield's $26,603. But it spends $70,316 because it can find it.

A clue to true costs surfaced in a 2006 investigation by Jonathan

Glater and Alan Finder in the *New York Times*. They had discovered that Pennsylvania's Ursinus College had decided to increase its fees by 17 percent, because it believed it wasn't getting enough applicants due to its modest sticker price. After all, behavioral economics posits that when people feel what's being asked is too low, they suspect something might be wrong with the product. Here, the economists were right; within four years, Ursinus enrollments had grown by a third. Glater and Finder found similar increases at Rice University, Hendrix College, and Bryn Mawr. These rises, they observed, "have helped produce an economy in academe something like that of the health care system, with prices rising faster than inflation." Actually, it's producing a system like the airlines, where one passenger pays twice the fare of the person in the adjacent seat. With almost every private college offering "discounts," and the "needy" defined as households with incomes as high as $180,000, a cottage industry of consultants has sprung up to advise parents on how to bargain with aid officers to maximize packages.

Let's go back for a moment to what good liberal arts colleges are charging. Here are a few more tuition prices for the 2008–9 academic year: Dartmouth College, $37,250; NYU, $37,372; Barnard, $37,538; Haverford, $37,525; Penn, $37,376; University of Chicago, $37,632; Williams College, $37,640; Mount Holyoke, $37,646; Pitzer College, $37,870; University of Southern California, $37,890. Notice anything odd? The margin of difference among them is less than 2 percent—1.7 percent, to be exact. Since these schools differ in characteristics and locales, what accounts for their fees being so close? Barnard and USC are urban, where expenses tend to run high, but Pitzer and Dartmouth are semirural. Williams has triple the per capita endowment of Mount Holyoke, yet their sticker prices are only six dollars apart.

No, we don't believe that presidents get together and agree on an acceptable range. Even so, like Hertz and Avis, they keep a constant watch on what their competitors are charging. But something more is at stake. It seems clear that Williams, which is amply endowed, could easily reduce its $37,640 fee down to, say, $17,640. But a consequence might be to lure applicants from a less affluent Haverford, which couldn't match Williams's lower price. So for all practical purposes, there seems to be something like a tacit agreement by rich schools not to undercut their poorer cousins. But self-interest is also at play. Were it to become known that a Williams education was costing only $17,640, to some people it would look more like a stripped-down car than a top-line model. Murmurs might be heard: could Williams be cutting corners? Insofar as a sticker price attests to the worth of a degree, which led Ursinus to raise its fees, the upshot is high prices across the board, followed by the minuet of negotiating discounts. Cooper Union admits all its students free of charge due to its generous endowment and ascetic ambience. Still, it wants its programs to be valued; so it lists its official tuition as $34,600, even though no one has ever paid it.

We may not ever completely know how final prices are arrived at, but we do have information on why they keep escalating. The big-ticket item at most colleges is faculty salaries, especially at tenured levels. Say good-bye to Mr. Chips with his tattered tweed jacket; today's senior professors can afford Marc Jacobs. After all, these are no ordinary employees; most have advanced degrees, and expect salaries commensurate with that status. Besides, parents wouldn't want their offspring to be taught by instructors with lesser credentials; college isn't high school. So it's not unusual for the adults in front of a classroom to receive more than $100,000 for an *annual* teaching schedule of three hundred hours.

In fact, until the recent financial crash, academic salaries had been rising at a much faster clip than in other occupations. Since the mid-1980s, as we have noted, full professors' pay at Stanford has increased 58 percent in constant dollars; at the University of North Carolina they are up 56 percent; and at Duke 65 percent.

Why have faculty salaries increased so markedly? The answer is simple; throughout the last several decades, the money has been there. Parents willingly paid the rising fees, alumni sent in donations, and colleges borrowed freely with distant payback dates. The idea also arose that the quality of a faculty could be gauged by how much its professors were paid. Outside observers may not understand what scholars do, but they can be impressed with six-figure salaries.

Thanks to tenure, faculty members can stay on the payroll as long as they like, with no real assessment of their performance. With lifetime assurances, professorships have become multimillion-dollar commitments.

If senior faculty take the most significant bite of a college budget, coming next is the ever proliferating bureaucracy. As discussed earlier, nowadays it isn't easy to show that education is the primary purpose of our colleges and universities. A head count at small Earlham College in Indiana shows that two-thirds of its personnel are engaged in activities other than instruction. At another liberal arts college, North Carolina's Davidson, less than a quarter are doing teaching. Of course, all these positions are claimed to "support" the academic side, as we're sure some librarians and lab technicians do. Walking across many campuses, one sees large numbers of adults: armies of administrative employees who almost overwhelm the students.

Most problematic from the cost point of view, once a new service is established, it—and the staff hired—can remain forever entrenched in the university's structure. Since 1976, the ratio of bureaucrats to students has literally doubled, contributing to a tandem rise in tuition fees.

College physical plants have become more expensive. Dormitories once provided double-deck beds, a military mattress, and a battered desk. Cafeterias offered a set menu: eat it or leave it. No longer. Students expect and get suites, private bathrooms, and food courts with specialized stations. So it should be no surprise that charges for room and board have also doubled in after-inflation dollars.

Of course, by many measures, students now get a lot more. Washington State University provides a jumbo Jacuzzi with room for fifty-three bodies, while the University of Houston sports a five-story climbing wall. College officials from all over the country have been visiting Kenyon to admire—with hope of emulating—its $70 million athletics center. Keeping up with the Kenyons is definitely one factor pumping up college costs.

The colleges are caught in an extravagant amenities race, tripping over each other to provide luxuries, large and small, especially aimed at seventeen-year-old applicants. At Bowdoin there's a chef who prepares butternut squash soup, Dijon chicken, and vegetable polenta for incipient epicures. Penn State leases a service allowing students to legally download music; at last count, they were acquiring two million songs a week. While visiting an Amherst dormitory, we saw free condoms available. Still, there was a sign: "Please don't take for solo sex!"

In academe, as in the corporate arena, executive compensation cannot be ignored. Between 1992 and 2008—that's only sixteen years—the salaries of most of the college presidents we looked at more than doubled in constant-value dollars. Some rose closer to threefold. (For a comparison, overall American earnings rose by 6 percent during this period.) The pay of Stanford's president increased from $256,111 to $731,614 in constant dollars, while that of NYU's president burgeoned from $443,000 to $1,274,475. The trend was similar at smaller schools. At Wellesley, Carleton, and Grinnell, presidential compensation rose from the low $200,000s to over $500,000.

In 2008, the most recent reports available show a dozen presidents receiving more than $1 million. Among them were the heads of Northwestern, Emory, Johns Hopkins, and the University of Pennsylvania. It's hard not to conclude that many colleges are emulating the corporate model: the stature of the enterprise is gauged by how much its top person is paid. Nor do we find signs that trustees and regents are objecting to this. The most frequently heard justification is that there's a shortage of executive talent, so you have to bid high to get and keep the best. Perhaps it was only a matter of time before this refrain, so popular in Wall Street and the Fortune 500, would reach the campus.

Some of the most innovative presidents we've come to know are on the lower end of the pay spectrum. When John Maeda took over at the Rhode Island School of Design, he actually gave back $100,000 of his salary for the students' scholarship fund. As we noted earlier, when Vartan Gregorian was offered Brown's top job, he didn't even bother to discuss pay with the trustees. By asking for what his predecessor was getting, "that meant the faculty couldn't use my compensation as an issue," he told us. "It gave me additional leverage and also—perhaps I was being selfish here— peace of mind." By contrast, we were struck by the triumphant tone of one of the highest-paid presidents we met at a meeting a few years back, who had reached seven figures at his not-quite-Ivy school. "For the first time," he quipped, "I'm getting more than the football coach." We tried to smile politely; after all, we were guests. But our hearts weren't in it.

Actually, he was acknowledging another secret of academic finance: football can be the biggest budget buster of them all. Every college head should repeat this maxim: football will almost always end up costing more than anything, whether library acquisitions or star professors. Even allowing for ticket sales, television revenues, and the hope of increased donations, the vast majority of varsity programs need to be subsidized from general college coffers. This is true of most football and basketball teams, which are supposed to turn a profit but hardly ever do. Two years ago, Eric Dexheimer of the *Austin American-Statesman* calculated that varsity sports at all colleges together run a deficit of $3.6 billion. Whether it's outlays for golf greens or hockey helmets, removing the athletics incubus would make attending college much cheaper.

Here's where money for athletics *does not* come from. It obviously can't be from current tuition receipts, which are used for salaries and mowing lawns. Even when there's a large donation, it's usually stretched out in installments. Arcane legal reasons make it difficult to borrow from the endowment. Rather, most of the structures seen rising on campuses are underwritten by bonds, which have an attraction for buyers because they are tax-exempt.

So almost every college carries a debt load. In 2009, Harvard's was $2.5 billion. Colgate's tax return, which we examined, showed indebtedness of $126 million. Even the Culinary Institute of America, which awards bachelor's degrees, is due to pay back $104 million. In 2009, Moody's estimated that higher education's total debt load is at least $170 billion. Annual interest payments must be remitted, and eventually the whole sum must be paid back. The profitable sports program at the University of Texas brings in $100 million each year. But $15 million of that goes out in debt service for stadium extensions and practice facilities. So debt is the 800-pound kangaroo on the quadrangle. Even as colleges face fiscal constraints, interest and principal payments legally take priority over other expenses. Or much worse. Norman Silber, a Hofstra law professor, warns that some colleges may "actually default and face foreclosures, repossessions, and in some cases, even bankruptcy."

Research conducted at colleges also adds to what parents pay. Conventional wisdom has it that grants are honeypots for the schools. Indeed, they sometimes are, in that as much as 50 percent is taken off the top for "overhead" costs.

Professors are expected to apply for funding that will cover equipment, travel, and often their own salaries while they're working on the project. But it doesn't always turn out that way. We discovered this when we heard Princeton's president, Shirley Tilghman, testifying before a congressional hearing on escalating tuition costs. She told the lawmakers a big reason for Princeton's increases came from its commitment to research. She mentioned the field of genomics, where its laboratories are doing pioneering work in metabolic homeostasis in yeast. Princeton reports that each year it spends $34,213 on research in the name of each of its students, but it receives only $17,318 in government grants and contracts for research, nowadays the primary source of funding. We're happy to stipulate that studies in metabolic homeostasis are important. But we don't think parents and students should have to pay for them by being sent higher tuition bills.

Here's something else that isn't in college catalogs. A big slice of the tuition pie ends up with lawyers and their clients. After hospitals, colleges may be our society's most sued institutions. Here are some reports that caught our attention.

- The University of Iowa paid $226,000 to a professor who said he had been falsely accused of altering student evaluations.

- A University of Florida dean, who had been charged with sending libelous e-mails, was given $517,000 to settle his claim.

- Two students who charged that they were sexually abused by Colorado football recruits received a joint award of $2.8 million.

- LaSalle University settled a suit brought by a family for $7.5 million, on behalf of their son, who sustained debilitating brain injuries while playing football for the school.

- A Charleston Southern professor, in a moonlighting stint, swindled local investors out of tens of millions; the university, which had been made a co-defendant, contributed $3.9 million toward the restitution.

We sometimes suspect litigants and lawyers are emboldened because they view colleges as easy marks, and are willing to settle rather than risk an embarrassing trial. We also wonder if some of these actions are brought because families expect schools to attend to everything and then are disappointed when they don't. Two of the cases we've cited would not have arisen if schools didn't have big-time football. Others were related to the tenure system, which we also want changed. For the rest, we'll only say that funding legal payments is hidden in tuition bills.

If college is so costly, how come 18,205,474 Americans are sitting in classrooms, and apparently paying their bills? One explanation is that students and their parents are finding ingenious ways to cobble together the fees. Another is that many have had to take out loans. We are a culture that, in the final analysis, really values higher education, and not, we think, entirely for material reasons. People are quite willing to mortgage their futures for it, often with noble intentions, but increasingly with parlous consequences.

In the past twenty or so years, as colleges have expanded their functions and raised their fees, educational leaders have tried to rationalize the new cost structure. William Bowen, a former president of Princeton, claims that "the number of students who are currently prevented from enrolling by a straightforward inability to pay is small." Part of his argument is that what's keeping them out is not insufficient funding but inadequate academic preparation. He's also saying that much of higher education is still relatively inexpensive. So we'll be discussing the array of options for pursuing a degree, and how people are paying.

Bowen spent much of his life at Princeton, and that may have skewed his perceptions. There and at other high-prestige colleges, a majority of students come from homes able to pay the full bills. So just because charges have been soaring, it doesn't mean they are beyond reach for everyone. Actually, a prime clientele for higher education has also been prospering. During the past several decades, the top economic tiers have been commandeering larger slices of the national income pie. In 2008, the most recent figures available as we write, the nation had over five million households with incomes over $200,000. Moreover, these groups are least affected by recessions. Insofar as many of these high-bracket families have children of college age, they hardly have to scrimp to send them away. So it shouldn't surprise us to learn that 58 percent of Yale parents can readily foot its full bill, as can 63 percent at Duke. Indeed, elite colleges rely on affluent applicants to sustain the cash flow they need. Despite talk of diversified admissions, year after year these schools end up taking the same proportion of full payers. Thus by chance or design, at least half of those they accept turn out not to ask for financial assistance, or even a discount on tuition. Of course, these top-tier households aren't typical. Still, they're an important part of the mix.

Every increase and amenity has been backed by the unspoken assumption that whatever the tab, someone will write a check, or use a credit card, or draw on a trust fund. Most notably, there has been a massive deployment of loans, a relatively recent development, which has brought colleges billions of additional dollars for their spending sprees. The earlier notion of promoting access by keeping costs down was lost in the swirl of big dollars, growing numbers of them borrowed.

When Gaston Caperton, the head of the College Board, was asked about graduates just entering their twenties who averaged $22,000 in loans—which meant many were a lot higher—he replied, "that's a pretty good investment for a student to make, when you consider it's about what you pay for a car." Nor did he remind us that sums like $22,000 are only the beginning. A public loan with a ten-year repayment for that amount will have $7,337 added in interest. Until 2010, many students were directed to private banks with twenty-year plans, so $29,999 would be added on. Thus their total wouldn't be the cost of a Honda, but more like a $50,000 Mercedes that Caperton might be driving. And despite legislative reforms, they will still have to finish paying at the private rates.

And it's the poor and working class who generally end up paying above the $22,000 average. At the urban University of Hartford, which serves many blue-collar and minority students, fully 78 percent graduate with debt, with a before-interest average of almost $39,000. Mississippi's Tougaloo College, a historically black school in the nation's poorest region, has 80 percent of its graduates holding loans, averaging $41,000. (Again: for upward of half, their debt is higher.)

And these are only for bachelor's degrees. Many will go on for graduate or professional study, so six-figure indebtedness will become extremely common. Due to the loan industry's lobbying, Congress obligingly decreed that student loans can never be discharged by bankruptcy. Higher education, which cheered on this borrowing to ensure its own cash flow, has created its counterpart of the housing bubble. Moreover, it was not unknown for financial aid officers to take payments for pushing students toward high-rate lenders. Officials at Johns Hopkins, Drexel, and the University of Texas, among others, were charged with having received stock or stipends as "consultants" or "advisors."

Late in 2009, a PBS *Now* program called "Student Loan Sinkhole" focused on Gina Moss, a Baltimore social services worker, whose life had fallen apart due to $70,000 in loans. Its website was inundated subsequently with recountings of similar stories. Here are a few extracts:

> *Monique:* I have about $100,000 in loans that I feel I will never be able to pay back. The phone calls don't stop. How do you juggle bills, car note, and insurance, and pay back what they demand on $40,000 a year? I'm back living with a parent. If I didn't have that, I'd be sleeping in my car.

Diana: My family always told me how important it is to finish college. I had some problems with a pregnancy, and wasn't able to work. When I contacted Sallie Mae, my principal had jumped from $42,000 to $63,000! I'm now current and slated to pay $460 until the year 2038!

Brenda: Even though I had cancer, I could not go into Chapter 7 on my student loans. They are enormous, and they even garnish my unemployment checks. I'll never be free of debt. Trying to go to college wasn't worth it.

So what are the options for young people who truly want an education? We think they should be smarter than the system that's purporting to serve them. The American way of higher education puts a premium on prestige, making a fetish of brand names and using price as a guarantor of quality.

There are better strategies. Some states actually have their own small liberal arts colleges—in a sense, public Amhersts and Pomonas. Thus there's New College in Florida ($4,046 for state residents) and Washington's Evergreen ($5,127). Somewhat more expensive are the University of Minnesota's branch in Morris ($10,312) and Maryland's campus in St. Mary's City ($11,989). But the best-kept secrets are others also like Amherst and Pomona, though in this case they are nestled within state schools otherwise known for their impersonality and big-time athletic teams. We're talking about public "honors colleges," which are relatively recent arrivals on the higher education scene. We've visited two of them, one at Arizona State University and the other at the University of Mississippi. We liked what we saw.

Arizona State's Barrett College, which enrolls 2,766 of the 30,363 overall undergraduate total, is self-contained with its own character and identity. It has its own dormitory and dining facilities, as well as special seminars and faculty advisors. Although its members take most of their classes in the general curriculum, they get preferred access in courses with limited places. They also get help with tuition and their living expenses if need can be shown. Barrett was established for a reason: to ensure there would be a pool of committed students within Arizona State, which otherwise takes almost everyone who applies. One such student is Michael McDowell, who combines dance and biochemistry majors. That may have been why he was accepted at Harvard, which he turned down because Arizona gave him a full financial package. "My father came from a very poor family and he made it on his own," Michael explained. "I don't really want to lean on him any more than I have to." Like many first-generation students, he wants to go to medical school. He won't have problems there, since Barrett has ensured he will be in upper-level courses with Arizona's top science professors.

The University of Mississippi (yes, "Ole Miss") has its Barksdale Honors College, taking in 860 members of the 9,200 undergraduate body. It offers perquisites much like Barrett's; indeed, state honors colleges keep in touch with one another. We were struck by its serious commitment to liberal education in the traditional mold. Dennis Pickens, who grew up in rural Lawrence County, also started with a vocational major—in his case, accounting. But Barksdale broadened that. "In two required seminars, we explored works like *The Communist Manifesto* and *The Screwtape Letters*," he told us. "When you think of an accounting major, you don't think of English or politics or anything like that." And like Barrett, Barksdale gives tuition remissions to out-of-state applicants, since it wants to expand its geographic and intellectual diversity. There will be more on these schools in a coming chapter.

Across the country, the largest group of undergraduates get their degrees from regional colleges within state systems. While the flagship University of Missouri enrolls 20,306 undergraduates, beneath the radar are another 78,881 students in twelve other branches: like Southern State in Joplin, Central Missouri in Warrensburg, and Northwest Missouri in Maryville. Indeed, regional colleges are where most of the nation's higher education takes place, and at relatively modest cost. True, attrition is high. But it's worth sticking it out.

We want to reiterate that you can get a very good liberal arts degree on these campuses. We've visited several, where we sat in on classes and conversed with faculty and undergraduates. We'll discuss one of these in greater detail in our final chapter, but two impressions stood out. First, the students are as bright and academically committed as any, and second, the regional professors are among the most dedicated we've met. At Western Oregon State in Monmouth, a one-traffic-light town, we spent a morning with Peter Callero and Dean Braa of the sociology department. They could speak to the talents and dreams of every one of their students, and talked about how much they liked teaching. In turn, several students we took to dinner expressed gratitude for the attention they were getting, a sentiment we didn't always encounter in our travels. They had high school friends studying at a much more impersonal Oregon State University. In their own view, they felt they were getting a far better education, in a more humane setting, at a considerably lower cost.

So it's possible to get a degree at relatively modest cost. Florida, for example, encourages students to start at one of its 28 community colleges, where yearly charges are as low as $2,086. Students who finish a two-year program there find it easy to transfer, and spend their junior and senior years at a full campus like Florida Atlantic, whose tuition is $3,782. The bare-bones four-year cost of a bachelor's degree is $11,736. Most American families could scrape this up; it's less than a stripped-down car. Of course, it assumes that you walk or bicycle to school, bring your own lunch, and live at home. Nor does it include forgone earnings, or textbooks and incidental supplies. And we'll be honest to say that not every state is as cheap as Florida. Up in New Hampshire, community colleges run to $5,730 a year, and the annual cost at Plymouth State University is $8,424, bringing a four-year total to $28,308.

Still, the bottom line rests with the College Board, which analyzed tuition costs at 672 public four-year institutions for 2008–9. The average sticker price was $6,600, which is a lot to ask from students of modest means. But the College Board also found that after Pell Grants and other assistance comes into play, the actual amount paid averaged $2,900, well under the published tab. We'd like to think most households could manage that kind of sum.

For most students the costs of instruction are not the main economic burden. What causes the cash crunch is that over half of public college students pursue their degrees at a distance from their homes. In other words, they "go away" to college, even if it's to miniscule Monmouth in Oregon. For them, the principal cost of education is not their classes, but living and dining in college housing or fraternities or sororities, or off-campus apartments. We have no firm figures on what living away costs, since they vary from bringing a new SUV with you to living on noodles and peanut butter. As one kind of index, schools publish their room and board charges, which run from $18,848 at Boston University to $3,800 at Blue Mountain College in Mississippi.

How much education is enhanced by living away from home has not been given serious study, although the accepted wisdom is that it must have good effects.

In some parts of Africa, when youngsters are about to come of age, they are taken to "adolescent huts," outside their villages, where they hear stories, sing songs, take part in rituals, and eventually emerge as full-fledged members of their tribe. In many ways, our sleepaway colleges serve a similar function, as they provide a place for young people to wean themselves from their parents and begin shaping their adult identities. Still, we often wonder if this high-priced interlude is worth the cost.

At least one of your authors doesn't think so; but he may be biased because he teaches at a commuter college. When he meets his students years after graduation, they seem just as cultured and socially adept as others he knows who went away. Of course, we can agree that living independently is a lot more enjoyable, and we're certainly not opposed to fun. Still, this chapter is about the costs of higher education, so we'd only say that the living-away experience is very expensive.

Most of us will agree that higher education brings benefits, whether as an economic investment or nourishing the mind. So we were surprised to find how little of their own money Americans are providing under that head. The Bureau of Labor Statistics conducts annual surveys of what households spend on what. So we examined those where one or both of the adults were between forty-five and fifty-four, a span where many have children of college age. In this cohort, the average income was $81,884, they own 2.3 vehicles, and spend $3,244 on eating out. Perhaps that's to be expected. But the most revealing finding for us was that personal outlays for education came to $2,012, well under what is paid for restaurant meals. Since this average is so low, it raises questions about how many parents are writing five-digit checks for their children.

Our best information on how much families are saving for college comes from a 2009 survey of students, conducted for the College Board. Only half of these young people said their parents had put anything aside; and in this group, half had banked less than $20,000. Due to this improvidence, even high-tier families are pleading near poverty—and getting a hearing. Princeton parents in the $125,000-to-$150,000 bracket now have to pay only half of their full bill. A major theme of college campaigns is that gifts support scholarships. What isn't said in the appeal letters is that six-figure parents are among the recipients.

We always like it when we hear of a college doing things right. Kwame Wright, an engineering student at Cooper Union, where everyone gets free tuition, told us he had been considering flying to Japan to take part in an international technology project.

"College has cost me nothing so far," he reasoned, "so why not take out a loan for the trip?" His advisor quickly scotched the idea: "You'll be much better off entering the workforce without any debts."

We wish other educators would be as responsible. Colleges should be helping to build the next generation's future, not mortgaging it.

· 8 ·

FIREPROOF: THE TANGLED ISSUE OF TENURE

At first glance, *tenure* seems an innocuous enough word. Literally, it refers to the period spent holding a position. As in, "His tenure as wrestling coach was the briefest in Yale's history." However, for professors, it may be the most important word in their vocational vocabulary.

And understandably so. For them, tenure is an ironclad assurance of lifetime employment. Once you have been given this guarantee, you can remain in your job for as long as you like. Even until you are well into your eighties; more than that, until the day you die. Of all the entitlements we cataloged in our opening chapter, tenure is the academy's counterpart of ascending Everest. Only one other occupation boasts such a bulwark: federal judges are also in their jobs for life.

So as we use the word, we want to emphasize that it is not just another faculty fringe benefit, like health insurance or long vacations. Nor is tenure simply another seniority system, like those embedded in union contracts and civil service rules. As we write these words in 2010, millions of Americans have lost their jobs and not found new employment, including many in professional fields. However, tenured professors are rarely downsized or discharged; the vast majority of them are, in a word, fireproof.

The only caveat is that their institutions remain solvent. Yet colleges are remarkably resilient; even during the depressed 1930s, hardly any closed down. In 2009 and 2010, when budgets had to be trimmed, staff cuts started at the bottom. Thus in California's public systems hundreds of contingent instructors were dropped; the classes they had taught were canceled and applying students were turned away. Some seniors couldn't find the courses they needed for graduation. But not one of their tenured professors was removed from the rolls. At worst, they suffered some unpaid furlough days, adding up to a single-digit pay cut.

Tenure is a tangled issue, evoking emotions on all sides. In particular, those who have this guarantee are well aware of how valuable their prize is. Nor are they short on arguments they hope will safeguard their security. Of course, the phrase most often heard is *academic freedom*. That, we are told, is what tenure is really all about.

Surely we all favor untrammeled inquiry, an unfettered pursuit of truth, the advance of knowledge both by scholars and teachers in the classroom. But, it is also added, tenure is not there primarily to benefit its holders. Rather, we hear, it is the larger society that needs professors to be protected, so the public as a whole can enjoy the fruits of their teaching and research. A 1974 New Jersey superior court decision is often cited. Tenure exists, it is said, out "of concern for the general welfare by providing the benefits of uninhibited scholarship and its free dissemination." Arguments like these can have a plausible ring, especially when they turn a professional perquisite into a national good. We hope we don't have to reiterate that we fully favor academic freedom, even granting, as we will see, that the phrase has many interpretations and applications.

Our question is whether tenure is what is needed to ensure its estimable and necessary blessing, or whether there might be better and more effective ways—at least some with fewer downsides. But first we will examine some of the real world costs and consequences when some 300,000 faculty members are cloaked with a guarantee of lifetime employment.

We realize that to question tenure puts us in strange company. Most of those who oppose it are executives who abhor employment guarantees of any kind, or conservatives who view it as the enabler of left-wing correctness on campuses. Our objections are based more on common sense than ideology. We want faculties to imagine new ways of organizing their jobs. So long as we have the lifetime safeguard, the centerpiece of academic culture will be the tenure quest and not the education of students or, indeed, the pursuit of knowledge undistorted by fears and careers.

Louis Menand, who teaches English at Harvard and writes regularly for *The New Yorker,* has said that academic freedom is "the philosophical key to the whole enterprise of higher education." We certainly share this view. In our understanding, it means research may be pursued without restraint and there must be no bars to exploring information and ideas in the classroom. Nor, we hear, can these guarantees be taken for granted. Many professors declare they need the lifetime guarantee because their efforts to pursue truth—and by extension their careers—are constantly under attack.

James Garland, who recently completed a decade heading Ohio's Miami University, says that when he meets with faculty, they still talk of "an increasing tendency of elected officials to try to rid universities of politically unpopular or controversial professors." He cites a faculty survey, admittedly conducted during the Clinton presidency, which found fully 37 percent saying they did *not* feel "free to express their ideas in class." He doesn't suggest that this kind of trepidation is less evident today. For our part, we wonder *what* it is that so many want to say while teaching their subjects, but forbear due to fear for their careers. And are these reasons for awarding lifetime employment to 300,000 other academics, including in astronomy? As we'll show, there are other, much better, safeguards for controversial teaching. We find the claim of public censure surprising because, as we've noted several times, the bulk of academic research is so arcanely expressed that it is beyond the grasp of outside audiences, even if they are college graduates. Most academics write and speak solely for their faculty peers, in a style and syntax akin to foreign languages. Today's social sciences consist mainly of mathematical models, and the humanities focus on poststructural analysis. Thus while most arts and sciences professors are progressive in their politics, they obscure their research with rubrics like *recursive textuality* and *heteronomous hegemony*. It's hard to imagine laypeople discerning threats to the status quo in such writings. Nor is it easy to visualize a conservative legislator brandishing a copy of *Semiotica*, which is the actual name of an academic journal.

We have scoured all the sources we could find, including the American Civil Liberties Union and the American Association of University Professors, yet we could not find any academic research whose findings led to terminating the jobs of college faculty members. We're referring to the research that chemistry professors do in chemistry, geologists do in geology, and English professors publish in literature. Tenure is meant to guarantee the integrity of research, but it's not clear that intellectual inquiry is what lifetime employment is protecting. Indeed, we're bemused that professors of mathematics also get the lifetime guarantee; is it because their theorems and equations might be seen as subversive? We'd be happy to be corrected if someone will show us some actual cases. Until that happens, we will argue that lifetime employment isn't needed to protect scholarship. Of course, there are intra-academic disputes—arguments over Plato or tectonic plates or the bombing of Nagasaki—that can become quite unpleasant. Here, too, as we'll show, there are better ways to cope with such quarrels than to guarantee lifelong livelihoods for several hundred thousand professors.

So for whom or for what is tenure protection still desired? Here are some actual cases:

- A professor at an Alabama college, when interviewed by a local newspaper, blamed its president for declining enrollment and poor student and faculty morale. He was subsequently dismissed for "malicious gossip and public verbal abuse."

- At a Baptist university in Ohio, a professor was discharged for failing to "maintain consistent, biblically appropriate, spiritual interest and effective Christian relations within the university family." The charges did not refer to his teaching or research, but informal expressions of his personal convictions.

- An engineering professor in Idaho, with twenty-two years on the faculty, incurred the wrath of his president by seeking a vote of no confidence for him. He was dismissed for "insubordination coupled with a complete lack of collegiality."

These cases have three common features. The first is that all three of the professors lost their jobs. The second is that all of them had been awarded tenure, so having that supposed safeguard didn't serve as a protection. The third is that none of their acts of speech and writing involved teaching or research in the fields where the professors had accredited competence.

Hence the question arises whether their *academic freedom* was threatened, and their jobs jeopardized, because of what might be called academic acts. It's true that they all held academic positions. But it's quite a stretch to say that because that is their occupation, everything they do must become an exercise of academic freedom. Criticism of a supervisor doesn't take on a special academic status because it is leveled at the head of a college rather than, say, an insurance company. We understand the desire of professors to be able to think and act freely and say what's on their minds, and we obviously support that wish. In fact, we engage in this ourselves.

We would only add that there are another three hundred million residents of this country who would also like to express themselves without hindrance or penalties. We hope it won't be argued that professors need broader and more vigorous protections for speech in and out of their workplace than accountants or dentists. When professors engage in extracurricular expression, stepping outside their classrooms and research sanctuaries, they should invoke the First Amendment, just like everyone else.

Now we want to turn to the final case on our list. It deserves to be examined in its own right. This is because it's the most prominent instance, since the McCarthy era, of a senior faculty member being dismissed by an important university. Ward Churchill was a tenured professor of ethnic studies, also chairing that department at the University of Colorado in Boulder.

The Churchill case wasn't an easy one for defenders of academic freedom. A theatrical figure who claimed American Indian descent, Churchill had written many books and articles in his academic field, with titles like *Struggle for the Land* and *Kill the Indian, Save the Man*. It certainly couldn't be argued he hadn't published. Like many professors, Churchill leaned toward the left and wasn't shy about airing his views. Indeed, his politics probably were helpful in getting him fast-tracked for tenure, after only a year on the full-time faculty. Colorado wanted a more pronounced presence in American Indian studies, and Churchill fit that bill. (The designation "Native American" is no longer used in academic circles.)

As is by now well known, the day after the World Trade Center was struck, Churchill wrote an article he called "Dark Night field notes" in which he described the victims as "little Eichmanns." Here are excerpts from that piece:

> As for those in the World Trade Center, they formed a technocratic corps at the very heart of America's global financial empire. If there was a better, more effective, way of visiting some penalty upon the little Eichmanns inhabiting the sterile sanctuary of the Twin Towers, I'd be really interested in hearing about it.

As is evident, his rationale for the Eichmann reference was that most of those who died worked in finance, and so were tacit collaborators in their country's aggressive designs. By any measure, this was a callous thing to say. (Many of the dead were busboys and firefighters.) As it happened, the book and article remained essentially unnoticed until 2005. But once the "little Eichmanns" passage surfaced and entered the public domain, the university was inundated with calls for Churchill's dismissal from almost every section of the country.

At issue was whether a university would stand behind a professor despite so much pressure for his immediate dismissal. Still, the chancellor of the Boulder campus and the elected board of regents agreed to announce—in many cases, grudgingly—that what Churchill had written was "constitutionally protected speech." (Nor was it remarked that what he said was outside his area of academic competence.) So he could not be discharged for his "little Eichmanns" statement. The University of Colorado has ambitions to build a national reputation. A precipitous firing would damage that effort. Interestingly, at that time, little was said about Churchill's possession of tenure.

Then the story took an unanticipated turn. In 2005, when the "little Eichmanns" quote was much in the media, a sociologist at a small Texas college contacted a *Rocky Mountain News* journalist, providing him with material alleging that Churchill's writings included fabricated and falsified sources. Soon articles on the charges appeared. University officials exclaimed they were shocked, or claimed that they were. True or not, the accusations had to be addressed. As it happened, back in 1996, a University of New Mexico professor had sent a Colorado dean a letter with similar charges about Churchill's work. People knew of its contents, but they weren't followed up. At that time, no need was felt to raise questions about Churchill. Now there was.

In accord with academic custom, several faculty committees were convened to gather facts and make recommendations. The panels, aware a broad public was watching, took up their tasks with vigor, down to scrutinizing every comma and semicolon of his published output. Their gleanings uncovered a host of problems that hadn't surfaced when Churchill had been awarded lifetime employment.

There were strong indications that he had appropriated the words and ideas of others without credit, and that he had distorted sources to make ideological points. It was even found that Churchill had arranged for a book he had written to come out under the name of another person, and that he then cited this volume to support his own statements in subsequent articles. The committee that conducted the most detailed investigation concluded: "The misconduct was serious, repeated, and deliberate." Of the nineteen professors on the three panels, all agreed that there had been research misconduct. Ten recommended that Churchill be allowed to stay on the faculty, but be suspended for a period of years; the other nine voted for his dismissal. The university administration, citing the misconduct finding but not the split on his removal, revoked his tenure and ordered he be terminated. The Colorado Regents upheld the administration's decision by an 8–1 vote. Both the faculty and officials who were involved insisted that falsification, fabrication, and plagiarism were the sole reasons for removing him from the university. Everyone who took part in the decision denied that his World Trade Center writing had colored or affected their determinations.

Churchill took his case to court. A lengthy trial heard forty-five witnesses, including the governor of the state, Churchill's out-of-state denouncers, and the professor himself. We've read the entire transcript, and thus have a fair idea of what the jurors heard. In the end, they found against the university, saying Churchill should be reinstated. They concluded it was his World Trade Center remarks, and not the research findings, that motivated the dismissal. Direct testimony and internal documents made it clear that a cadre of administrators and regents had wanted to dismiss him from the start, without hearings or proceedings. So the newspaper revelations about his research gave these officials an easier option. (We found ourselves recalling *Murder in the Cathedral*: "Who will rid me of this troublesome priest?")

The jurors rejected many pleas from the university's attorneys to take notice of whether Churchill had committed scholarly improprieties. Contributing to that position was their learning of the opening statement by one of the faculty bodies that had been appointed to examine accusations concerning his research.

> Before addressing directly the contents of those allegations, the Investigative Committee notes its concern regarding the timing and, perhaps, the motives for the University's decision to initiate these charges at this time.

Even so, this wasn't the last word. A month later, the trial judge vacated the jury's verdict; and later an appellate judge confirmed the reversal, asserting that because the university was an agency of the state, its decision could not be legally challenged. As we write, Churchill's lawyers are making a higher appeal.

Here's something we found, which the jury never heard. At

the University of Colorado, investigations of faculty research have been extremely rare. While there is a "standing committee" for that purpose, in the sixteen years from 1989 to 2005, only five cases had been referred to it, and in four, the decision was to take no action. With the fifth, the professor was found guilty of research misconduct but was not dismissed.

Since Churchill was, we wondered why his case was decided differently, or at least what the university would say. As it happened, a bit later we found ourselves at a dinner with Philip DiStefano, Colorado's chancellor and an important figure in the Churchill proceedings. When we asked about the divergent outcomes in the two cases, he told us that the earlier professor had expressed "remorse," whereas Churchill continued to deny he had committed any offenses. This seemed to say that had Churchill shown penitence, he would have been kept on the faculty.

In retrospect, we wished we had asked DiStefano another question. Churchill's work had come under scrutiny only because of outside reports, in this case newspaper stories. And the university wanted to show that research integrity matters a lot at Colorado. So, we've wondered, did the university consider announcing that it would like to hear from anyone who might have doubts about the scholarship of any of its 993 other professors?

We have given this much space to the Churchill case because it shows that possessing tenure is a feeble shield. If a college wants to oust a professor, it will do so, with or without rationalizations, even if it has to mount charges on an entirely different matter.

That was made plain during the McCarthy era. Being summoned to a legislative committee and then hounded to name associates who may have been Communists was the ritual that often ended with firings and sometimes prison sentences. So did having tenure protect professors when they refused to cooperate with investigating committees? A succinct answer has been given by Lionel S. Lewis, a sociologist at the University of Buffalo. "Faculty with tenure appointments were fired with nearly the same abandon as those without tenure," he wrote of the McCarthy period in his classic book, *Cold War on Campus.* "The message from academic authorities was indisputable: we reserve the right, when the chips are down, to renege on tenure rules."

We recently asked Lewis to look back in his files on the 1950s and identify for us some of the institutions that fired professors who were ostensibly tenured. His list included Tulane, Temple, Reed, Fisk, New York University, and Jefferson Medical College, as well as public universities in Ohio, Vermont, Minnesota, and Kansas. At the University of California, there were forced resignations. Rutgers permitted a tenured faculty member to "resign before being terminated." A half-century later, the University of Colorado can be added to the McCarthy era list.

So tenure isn't a protection when it's really needed. But something else is important. The protection, insofar as it is that, *only* covers those who have been elevated to the tenured tier. In most of our colleges and universities, it is the assistant professors, adjuncts, lecturers, and graduate assistants who do the bulk of the teaching and at least a share of the research. At most schools, one gets the feeling that the senior professors couldn't care less about the intellectual freedom of these lesser beings. In any case, tenure isn't a guarantor of academic freedom—whether construed broadly or narrowly—nor should it be expected to be. What is needed are presidents and trustees with the backbone to defend not just full professors but part-time adjuncts who raise the ire of outside critics.

During the McCarthy era, Robert Hutchins of the University of Chicago and Harold Taylor at Sarah Lawrence College stood behind faculty members who refused to cooperate with legislative inquiries, while their peers at Harvard and Columbia let those committees call the tune. So today we want to tip our hats to Martha Gilliland, who stood up for academic freedom against a set of facts as challenging as those in the Ward Churchill debacle.

In 1999, a political scientist who had a specialty in gender studies at the University of Missouri in Kansas City published a scholarly article in the *Journal of Homosexuality*. It adhered to the standard academic format, replete with footnotes, references, quotations, and citations. Though the piece wore its ideology openly—"sexuality became a weapon of class warfare"—it appeared in a peer-reviewed journal within the author's discipline. We mention all this because its subject was one that was guaranteed to give any university administrator a coronary: pedophilia.

The author argued that though the practice was now regarded as "unnatural," it might someday lose that designation, just as our understanding of the "natural" role of women had altered and views of gays and lesbians were changing. Not surprisingly, the article came to the attention of the *Kansas City Star*, and then the Missouri legislature, where some chose to see it as being a disguised defense of child molestation. Soon there were calls for the professor to be fired. The lawmakers settled for docking the university $50,000, an amount equivalent to nearly half the professor's pay and benefits. But throughout, Chancellor Gilliland never buckled. She got the backing of the University of Missouri state system and then told the world, "Our faculty have a right to conduct research, publish their findings and exercise free speech," adding, "The integrity of our educational systems depend on it."

What we also find significant is that Gilliland never mentioned that the professor had tenure, which he did. To do that would have focused on his privileged status, rather than a principle. More than a decade later, Gilliland told us, "Tenure was beside the question; that's why I never raised it. Nor was it about whether one condones certain behavior, it's about whether this was legitimate research."

Looking back, this administrator has no regrets about her actions. "There was no question I should stand up," she says. "I would rather lose my job." If tenure were removed, freedom of inquiry would depend on whether academic leaders were willing to emulate her example. But if tenure is preserved and Martha Gilliland is an exception, we can expect more cases like the one involving Churchill and Colorado.

If, as we argue, tenure is not required for academic freedom, it loses the strongest argument on its side of the balance sheet. So now we want to turn to the consequences of bestowing employment guarantees on a critical mass of faculty members. In our view, the costs outweigh the benefits, indeed, eclipse them entirely, since we're hard-pressed to identify any when it actually does protect intellectual inquiry.

To start, tenure creates an inverted pyramid, with safeguarded senior professors far outnumbering their junior colleagues. Indeed, throughout the country, the percentages are strikingly similar. At Berkeley, 77 percent of the full-time faculty have permanent appointments, as have 76 percent at the University of Pennsylvania. At Pomona College, 73 percent are tenured, with Williams just behind at 72 percent. Top-heavy faculties are equally evident in regional colleges. At Wisconsin's Lacrosse State University, 72 percent are in for life, as are 71 percent at California's Chico State. Due to these figures, and because senior professors are highly paid, little is left in faculty budgets to bring along junior people. At Stanford University, only 16 percent of its payroll dollars are left for lecturers and assistant professors. As a result, young teachers and scholars can't start their careers, since those in the tenured tier don't have to retire.

Thus in 2009 and 2010, when California's university systems faced financial shortfalls, it was instructors, adjuncts, and graduate assistants whose jobs were cut. "We simply have less money," announced Claudia Mitchell-Kernan, a UCLA vice chancellor. "Our priority is regular faculty who have tenure and need to be paid." So they get first call on whatever funds are available, regardless of their contribution to the curriculum. And it was students who truly suffered, since classes they needed were cancelled, not least because contingent faculty had been teaching many of the required courses.

This has moral implications. Every college has senior professors who keep on enjoying generous salaries and light teaching loads. Even so, they refuse to step aside, perhaps because they like their corner offices or holding forth at meetings—or even because they rightly dread the loss of status that the designation *retired* implies. What they will not admit is that their preemption of payroll funds leaves little to hire young people who are coming along. Nor do they feel any obligation to make what, yes, would be something of a sacrifice. The academic world has always said that it adheres to higher standards than profit margins and bottom lines. Tenure brings out tendencies that belie this claim.

Tenure might cause fewer problems if professors who have it were as mobile as other Americans. But once they get the award, most hunker in and never leave. At three colleges we sampled—Colby, Middlebury, and Reed—fully two-thirds of their faculties had been there for at least twenty years, and it seemed clear that most of them would be remaining until they decide to retire. The principal reason they stay is that few of them receive overtures from other colleges. After all, once they get tenure, they no longer have to worry about gaining or maintaining national reputations. Many won that safeguard in less stringent days, when being a congenial colleague was enough. In those palmier times, as William Rice, who teaches English at Kennesaw State University, put it to us, departments were "willing to tenure anyone who had not thrown chairs at students."

The very presence of tenure makes it the central social marker on campuses. For younger academics, the rituals involved in achieving it become the focus of their lives.

After Amy Bishop, the University of Alabama at Huntsville

biologist who is alleged to have opened fire on the academic committee that denied her tenure, the educational press was full of expressions from professors complaining of the "stress" of the process. "When a faculty member is turned down for tenure, would it be possible to have a senior colleague (probably outside the department) offer to provide regular support and contact for that person during their final year?" suggested one correspondent on the *Chronicle of Higher Education*'s blog. "I would guess that the experience of being turned down for tenure, the profound anxiety of wondering if your entire career has come to an end, and the terrible, terrible isolation that must inevitably follow from that experience would be almost overwhelming for any of us."

One thing is certain: the tenuring process actually discourages intellectual audacity among the hopeful. Just as students who scramble for high grades lose out on authentic learning, scholars on the tenure quest calculate their careers, which trumps risky creativity. Though the stated rationale for tenure is the protection of free inquiry, the demeanor required to obtain it depends heavily on caution. To get past a tenure committee, assistant professors are increasingly expected to produce at least one book, several scholarly articles, present papers at conferences, teach large introductory courses, and perform "service" to their institution, the last mainly by sitting on committees.

During what is commonly a six- or seven-year probation, few junior faculty are willing to try unconventional research or break with the orthodoxies of their discipline, espouse dissenting ideas, indeed do anything that might otherwise displease their seniors. "The doctoral student and the assistant professor are free to write what they choose," Louis Menand says, but then adds, "What they write had better accord with their senior colleagues' idea of what counts as scholarship."

Nor is it all about the life of the mind. We know of a young social scientist at an unprepossessing college in New Jersey. In his fifth year on the track, very close to the "brass ring," as it's been called, he was urged by his elders to serve on no fewer than ten different committees. It was, he said, akin to a fraternity house ritual, to prove his willingness to fulfill the "service" test. Though most of these panels were a patent waste of time, he didn't dare say no. "I'm up for tenure next year," he told us, as if the phrase explained everything. "I wouldn't want to seem uncollegial."

Indeed, the tenure hurdle can actually undercut the kind of work colleges are supposed to do. A young professor in biochemistry told us self-censorship was especially evident when junior faculty work under senior people, because junior scholars may hesitate to point out errors or misinterpretations of data. Although some mentors are secure enough to take such comments in good spirit, the young professor we spoke with has witnessed enough rankled reactions to suggest that silence may be the best counsel. The bottom line, she said, is that science suffers. Of course, people would still worry about careers if tenure didn't exist. But when all of your prospects hinge on that single decision, the anxieties can only worsen, with consequences for scholarship as a whole.

The tenured tier not only decides who will be allowed to join them, but they fill the junior positions as well. Given their advancing years, they tend to be conservative—even if ideologically liberal—and look for colleagues with whom they will feel comfortable. "The academic profession," Louis Menand has observed, "is not reproducing itself so much as cloning itself." Nor is the worry simply brash personalities; new ideas they find hard to understand can also be unsettling. To this we'd add that most of those with permanent appointments are Caucasian by genetics and male by gender. So we'd simply add that warm welcomes have not exactly been extended to women and candidates of non-Caucasian origins.

With women, we'll start with a simple fact. For at least thirty years, women have been awarded over half of all bachelor's degrees, the first step for professional careers. And among the PhDs granted in 2008, the most recent figures as we write, women accounted for 63 percent in literature, 73 percent in psychology, and are making strides in the sciences, with 51 percent in biology. The good news is that, apart from the physical sciences, they are coming close to parity in assistant professor appointments. At Harvard, they hold 49 percent of these tenure-possible positions. At Michigan State, it is 45 percent. Their numbers are also climbing at the associate level. But it remains to be seen how far they will ascend to full professorships. Currently, they hold only 21 percent at Michigan State and 27 percent at Harvard. So it would seem there are a lot of women in the proverbial pipeline. Still, as we've noted, senior men are in no hurry to retire, and their places can't be filled until they do.

The statistics are even worse for non-Caucasian males. Even now only 6 percent of full professors are of African, Hispanic, or American Indian heritage. Troy Duster, a Berkeley sociologist, has found that though senior professors disclaim any bias, their values have the same effect. "Hiring committees often believe they are upholding the values of Western culture," he told us. "So when new groups come in, they feel challenged."

We have interviewed, or simply chatted with, literally scores of accomplished professors. Since we knew we'd be writing this chapter, we asked them if their lifetime employment guarantee enhanced their academic performance. Sometimes we got an indulgent smile; at others, something closer to a snort. They uniformly told us, of course it didn't improve their work; moreover, they didn't need it. They knew what they were doing was important, that they were doing it well, and their colleges appreciated their contributions. These are the faculty members schools want to keep; indeed, are afraid of losing. Giving them tenure, if they didn't already have it, would hardly figure in deciding whether to go or stay.

In fact, staying for life is more likely to saddle a faculty with a "percentage of professors," as James Garland puts it, "who haven't had an original idea in years, and who put forth the bare minimum of effort in their classes." We heard as much from students. A young woman at Arizona State University told us of a political science professor who surprised his students on the first day of class by announcing, "I have tenure, so I can teach you or not teach you, you're the ones who have to take the tests."

His smugness came from his confidence that he could stay on as long as he wasn't found guilty of financial improprieties, sexual harassment, or egregious research misconduct. Would he have been a better teacher if he didn't have tenure? Given his attitude, we're not ready to say that. But if he had a contract—renewable, say, every six years—we suspect he would have invested more of himself in his classes and students.

In theory, there's a mechanism for getting rid of underperforming faculty—it's called "post-tenure review." The concept looks good on paper, which undoubtedly was its purpose. Indeed, most public systems have such procedures; the question is how they are used. In Arizona, reviews of 2,711 professors found only four unsatisfactory. Texas scrutinized an even larger number, but called for only one revocation. In Massachusetts, Indiana, and Georgia, everyone examined got clean bills of health.

At the University of Maryland, as reported in *Inside Higher Ed*, it was proposed that tenured professors whose work was found to be "substantially below reasonable and equitable expectations" would have to submit a "personal development program." The faculty overwhelmingly rejected the idea. The objections were what one would expect: professors would give out higher grades and substitute entertainment for enlightenment. Some dismissed it as a nuisance. "Preparing material for a committee," Gay Gullickson, a history professor, said, "would take more time away from scholarship and teaching."

Student reaction is different. After all, they're being taught by tenured professors. In talking with undergraduates, we've found them angry that there's nothing they can do about bad tenured teaching. From Arizona State to Harvard, students have told us,

"They're tenured—what can we do?" What they get is a lesson in powerlessness. Anupama Kothari, a student government leader at the University of Maryland, asked them, "If you are doing a good job, why are you so scared of being reviewed?"

We certainly support warnings and self-help efforts. We'd only add it may be a formidable task, especially for senior faculty who have been honing their imperfections for thirty years. But post-tenure scrutiny seldom gets beyond promises of reform. "The schools don't dismiss people because of the fear of litigation," notes Peter Byrne, professor of law at Georgetown and chair of the tenure committee. "It's very expensive and drawn out; bringing a case to decision can be ruinous. It doesn't happen much."

This ends our bill of particulars. To allow so significant a stratum of employees this unique status subverts the very enterprise they are supposed to serve. Lifetime security cannot be shown to be needed for, let alone enhance, good teaching or research. On the contrary, it diminishes both those endeavors. So we will be proposing that one of the most important reforms higher education can institute is to start moving away from tenure and begin experimenting with other systems of employment.

But first a word on retirement. We're wary of systems that set a specified age. We oppose age discrimination in every segment of society. But the problem takes another turn when age gets mixed with the lifetime guarantee. Simply stated, a lot of people who should be retiring refuse to do so. Were tenure to be eliminated, decisions could be made on a case-by-case basis, as happens in other employment settings. We know of many senior professors who perform as well, and sometimes better, as their junior colleagues. So we can see why vibrant and productive men and women would not want to be confronted with compulsory retirement. There are academic counterparts of Justice John Paul Stevens, of the U.S. Supreme

Court, who could write a cogent ninety-page opinion on the eve of his ninetieth birthday.

There are other options. Middlebury College in Vermont has an original and sensible solution that appears to work well. After their professors reach the age of sixty, they can shift to "associate status." Under this title, they teach every other semester, plus a short intersession, for which they receive about three-fifths of their former salary, along with the customary benefits. They are freed from committee chores and can keep their offices, although they may share it with a visitor during their off-semesters.

John Berninghausen, a professor of Chinese, told us why at the age of sixty-four he decided to move to associate status for five more years. "First, my children had finished college, our mortgage was fully paid, and we could live quite nicely on a somewhat smaller salary, until my pension starts," he said. "Also, I wanted to quit at the top of my game. It wasn't that my powers were ebbing, but I will have had thirty-seven good years at Middlebury and that seemed a respectable stint." He then added, "So I suppose Oprah Winfrey and I have something in common." We wish that more professors would be as wise and self-effacing as John Berninghausen.

There's another possibility at Middlebury. Retired professors who have shifted fully to pensions can teach one course per semester, often filling in for people on leave. The stipend isn't huge, so they don't do it for the money. It's because they like keeping active, and teaching young people isn't a bad way to stay on your toes.

We'd like to think that removing the lifetime vise would enable more professors to adapt their careers to changing times and conditions. Plus, as we feel we must reiterate, to look within and decide to do the right thing.

Simply stated, our alternative to tenure is some variant of a contract system, with, say, a five- or seven-year term and of course renewable. This would ensure a secure interval, allowing for periodic reassessments. Nor is this some utopian dream. Hampshire College in Massachusetts and Shenandoah University in Virginia are private schools, both of which attract good professors without a lure of lifetime guarantees. Evergreen State College in Washington and Florida Gulf Coast University have made the same decision. We've visited the latter two and were impressed with the quality and commitment of their faculties. Our point is that it's altogether possible for higher education to function like other professions. As we've noted, the best professors feel no need for total security. They are good; they know they are; and they know that others know. We sometimes wonder if tenure hasn't become a haven for academics of middling, even dubious, competence.

At Evergreen, an experimental public college, there are strong contractual protections against arbitrary firings, accompanied by periodic faculty evaluations. We talked with Stephanie Coontz, who teaches history and sociology and subjects in between, since Evergreen has no departmental boundaries. "Doubtful teachers are given the chance to hear what's missing in their performance and improve in a team-teaching experience," she told us. "Deans and colleagues look at evaluations, syllabus, even papers your students have written." Ms. Coontz—Evergreen also has no professorial ranks or titles—is the author of several books and very much a star at Evergreen. But she's not excused: "I have an evaluation conference coming this spring."

Over in New England, at Hampshire College, new faculty are hired on a three-year contract, then another for four years, and after that there's a ten-year review. Their president, Ralph Hexter, told us that even without tenure, they don't have much turnover. "Though some people think we have flexibility, it hasn't turned out that way," says Dr. Hexter, chuckling. "It's rare that people are not renewed; once someone has gotten a ten-year contract, it would have to be gross malfeasance to remove them." NYU's

School of Global Liberal Studies is a kind of in-house arts and sciences college, where faculty contracts are renewable every three years. Because teaching is the main consideration, student evaluations play a larger role than at the rest of the university. Yet judging by the manifestos decorating offices, the level of intellectual freedom seems quite robust. Indeed, some of the faculty backed the union efforts of adjuncts and graduate assistants, opposing the official university stance. This lively atmosphere reinforces our view that intellectual freedom on a campus depends more on the political climate of the time—or the region—than on tenure.

If professors see themselves facing an autocratic management, let's recall that insofar as tenure helps, it's only for the privileged tier that has it. Moreover, there are other ways to confront despotic deans. Academics could still form unions, strengthen professional associations, and get engaged with lawmakers and outside groups to win support for their positions. A good beginning would be to press Congress to override the Supreme Court's 1980 *National Labor Relations Board v. Yeshiva* decision, which oddly decreed that at private colleges, all professors belong to management, so administrations do not have to recognize faculty unions. Moreover, professors could still hire lawyers—something they do regularly now—if they felt they were unjustly treated. Indeed, some courts have reversed tenure rejections and could do the same for unrenewed contracts.

Demographics and economics tell us tenure is already under pressure. The big question is how or whether senior slots will be replaced. At this point, the hiring of on-track assistant professors hasn't diminished, although we'll have to see how many will be lofted up.

"Tenure will become a less prevalent practice," Harvard's Richard Chait told us, "as one position at a time is reclassified from tenure to non-tenure, from full-time to part-time. Grain by grain, the tenure shore is being eroded."

So when some tenured professors finally retire, their salaries will be divided up to hire a retinue of underpaid adjuncts. If academics themselves don't start proposing alternate modes of employment, cries of economic stringency may end up replacing tenure with something far more industrialized and inhumane than what we have now.

· 9 ·

THE ATHLETICS INCUBUS

Did you know that MIT has a football team?

Yes, each autumn the nation's preeminent science and engineering university garbs fifty-six players in cardinal and black jerseys to meet rivals like Massachusetts Maritime, Framingham State, and Salve Regina University. The team is supervised by eight salaried coaches, is publicized on a twenty-page website, and claims it supports itself on an annual budget of $111,203. (Women's rowing at MIT admits to $223,922.) Between 2004 and 2008, it racked up fourteen wins and thirty-two losses.

Though MIT's public relations office churns out tidbits about the "Engineers," as they are called, its 4,138 undergraduate students display little interest in their team. At a typical home game, only 683 spectators are in its stadium. The NCAA, which keeps records on this, notes that MIT placed 208th in attendance of 236 Division III teams. (The schools ranking below it have much smaller enrollments.) We once asked Susan Hockfield, MIT's president, why they even bothered with football. She hesitated and then murmured something about building school spirit, but clearly was uncomfortable with the issue. We forbore from asking if she attends.

Welcome to the world of self-delusion and magical thinking that shrouds much of intercollege athletics. We call this chapter "The Athletics Incubus" after the demons of myth, those evil spirits that descend on sleeping persons (or, in this case, institutions) and create havoc with their beings. America's colleges were founded to educate its young, to pass on the wisdom of previous generations, and to extend the range of human knowledge. College athletics originally came into the campus as an innocent form of recreation and diversion. Yet over the years the athletics incubus has overtaken academic pursuits, compromised the moral authority of educators, and gobbled up resources that should have gone to their basic missions.

We intend to argue that the virus is endemic, infecting almost all of the 1,057 colleges that sponsor varsity teams. And while it is easy to cite differences between programs, there are also striking similarities, and these are what we will be stressing. Here are vignettes of two schools, both of which in their own ways take intercollegiate competition very seriously.

The University of Texas is a major athletic power. In 2008, it reported spending $100,982,596 on its sixteen varsity teams. Revenue from football recoups most of that outlay, since it sells 98,046 tickets at a typical home game, including to undergraduates who pay through a compulsory athletics fee. In all, 525 students play on Texas teams, with 143 signed up for football or basketball, almost all of them especially recruited. But since there are 36,835 undergraduates, it means that only 1.4 percent of them participate in varsity programs. Nor has Texas shown interest in raising that ratio. Its aim is top rankings for its two high-profile sports.

Although Williams College in Massachusetts has fewer than two thousand students, it fields twenty-eight teams, ranging from ice hockey and water polo to golf and alpine skiing. It also sponsors football, with ten salaried coaches, outnumbering its physics department's eight professors. Altogether, 793 men and women, fully 40 percent of its student body, play on its varsity squads. Applicants with an aptitude for, say, water polo have an edge in the admissions process, especially if the coach puts in a good word. Williams reports spending $4,217,896 annually on intercollegiate athletics, with hardly any recouped.

We have decided not to dilate on the scandals, corruption, and arrogance infecting high-powered athletics. They include players prone to sexual assaults, coaches skirting rules to sign up stars, professors passing absent athletes, and alumni ready with backdoor bribes. Armloads of books have been written about the corrosive effects of commercialization and striving to win no matter what. So we won't try to echo Murray Sperber's *Beer and Circus: How Big-Time College Sports Is Crippling Undergraduate Education* or William C. Dowlings's *Confessions of a Spoilsport*, both of which we warmly recommend. Our chief concern is with how the incubus has been spreading, in overt and subtle ways, to what are otherwise respected centers of learning.

In 2008, the most recent figures at this writing, the 1,057 colleges sponsored a total of 17,917 teams that had 418,345 undergraduates on their rosters. Here are some salient features of intercollegiate— sometimes called varsity—athletics:

- Whether at the University of Texas or Williams College, the students who join varsity teams are designated as *athletes*. That's how the admissions office sees them, how their classmates generally view them, and how they tend to regard themselves. NCAA officials in far-off Indianapolis make rules about their hours of practice, when coaches can contact their parents, how much pocket money a college can give them. Even if they don't receive scholarships for playing, their sport becomes their principal activity and has first call on their time. A Harvard sophomore told us he thought he would like to try his hand at baseball. The coach was sympathetic, but told him that all the team's places had been filled with specially recruited players. Indeed, they had been early identified by the athletic staff, with their names flagged for the admissions office. In this, Harvard isn't wholly different from big-time bowl contenders.

- Student athletes are trained and recruited by salaried coaches, who oversee players on a daily basis and decide their deployment on the ice or court or field. It is an intensive relationship; indeed, one more direct and demanding than most students have with their professors.

- Teams compete against other colleges, accompanied by the expense of travel, sometimes to distant states, which can run to chartered planes and hotel accommodations, not to mention that players may miss successive classes.

- A team is expected to rack up more victories than defeats, a goal not easily attained when every match has a loser. This explains the ever-rising salaries of coaches. Mack Brown, who directs Texas's football program, gets $5 million annually in hope that he will continue a winning streak.

  Nor is generosity only at the top. Ed Orgeron, Tennessee's assistant defensive football coach, receives $650,000. Of course, such paychecks no longer shock at schools where sports are unabashedly a business. Still, the pay-for-winning sentiment seeps down, even to a sport like ice hockey, which is not expected to turn a profit. An NCAA study found that half its coaches are paid at least $252,000, over twice the salary of professors at most institutions.

- The overwhelming majority of those 17,917 teams in all sports and schools end up losing money. In the top football division, which can count on strong ticket sales, 113 of its

118 teams still run a deficit. Of the five that made a profit, only two brought in enough to erase the overall deficit of their schools' athletics departments.

- College sports are akin to an arms race: once started, they create their own momentum. Anthony Marx, the president of Amherst, once suggested to some of his fellow liberal arts college presidents that they borrow a practice from international diplomacy, an athletics equivalent of mutual arms reduction. He'd downsize Amherst's money-eating football program if others followed suit. It was as if Marx, a political scientist, had asked North Korea to dismantle their SCUD missiles. He had no takers.

- Colleges create teams, not necessarily because students want them but for circuitous reasons. Ohio State has a preponderance of male athletes, largely the doing of its humongous football squad. So it installed women's rowing to get closer to a gender balance, as decreed by Title IX. A problem: few high schools sponsor this sport, and no women were signing up. Amanda Purcell, a music major, caught a coach's eye due to her sturdy 5-foot-9 frame. In return for pulling an oar, the college is paying her full tuition, plus $10,800 toward room and board. But since not enough others followed her, the team decided to recruit from abroad. In Ohio State's lead boat are five rowers from Germany, one from Russia, and another from the Netherlands. Did the original authors of Title IX envision their egalitarian measure as creating educational opportunities for female athletes from Europe?

Now to those myths and mantras, contending that varsity sports are a positive force. We'll try to show how they are thin on evidence and rely on assertion in lieu of analysis.

Myth: Intercollegiate competition builds school spirit.

Reality: On an autumn afternoon, upward of 30,000 Ohio State students are among the more than 100,000 spectators cheering their team on against the University of Michigan. We'll agree their presence is evidence of their pride in being Buckeyes, especially because they usually win. (We might add that OSU undergraduates don't get in free; those who want to cheer their team must buy a $150 five-game package.) Nor are we so naïve to suppose that these students would be equally aroused if their college reached the finals in a regional chess tournament. Still, if spirit is seen as a good thing, we want to take a closer look at what this pride is about.

On a football field, defeating Michigan shows Ohio State has displayed its superiority, at least in a stadium. But by almost all other measures, Michigan is a better school. In *U.S. News & World Report*'s 2010 ratings of public universities, it was ranked fourth, only behind Berkeley, UCLA, and Virginia. Ohio State, on the other hand, was eighteenth, following twelve other state schools, including Florida and Georgia Tech. True, there has been criticism of the rankings; still, athletic prowess isn't in the equation. The two states are comparable in size and economic standing, and they seem equally willing to invest in football. But there the resemblance ends. Michigan has built highly regarded medical and law schools, while Ohio's are clearly lower tier. Michigan seeks to attract and keep a quality faculty, plus its students' SATs average 1375 against 1200 for Ohio State. In fact, OSU's students and alumni know their university runs a poor second to Michigan by any academic reckoning. That they look for redress on a football field strikes us as a trifle sad.

We've found that at colleges where the students are pleased with the educations they're getting, they feel little need for varsity competition to pump up school spirit. Indeed, it bemuses us why so many colleges continue with costly football squads when so few of their students seem to care. We've already noted of MIT's

4,138 undergraduates, only 683 are at an average game. At Grinnell, a well-regarded liberal arts college, 411 of its 1,623 students typically turn out. And of the 6,467 enrolled at St. Louis's Washington University, 5,250 are somewhere other than the stadium on a Saturday afternoon. These small turnouts lead us to suspect that at these schools and elsewhere, students have found other ways to express pride in their schools.

Myth: Enrolling athletes creates a more diverse campus.
Reality: An earlier myth, now mercifully retired, was that recruiting black students for varsity teams allowed them to continue their education and leave with degrees. We hardly hear this argument anymore, since it's understood that the only reason most of them are on the campus is to play. Football and basketball in particular demand so much time and energy that it's almost impossible to carry a serious academic program—all the more if you come with marginal preparation. At some schools, graduation rates have been in the single digits. Black athletes, more than others, are fodder for coaches, to use when they're needed and discarded when they're not. It's not inherently racial; some young African Americans simply have the skills coaches seek. If colleges found that mathematics championships could make money, we'd see students of Asian and Russian origin being avidly recruited.

We'll grant that having a basketball team composed almost entirely of black players will help integrate a mostly white campus. But the numbers are usually modest. Of the twelve members of the Rutgers 2009 women's squad, eleven were of African-American origin and had been recruited from as far as California and Mississippi. But since Rutgers has 26,479 students, it's unlikely those eleven faces add much to their diversity. Most of the 628 colleges fielding football, and the 1,954 with basketball, don't have the budgets or reputations needed for scouting inner-city talent. Even with high-powered Duke's basketball, the roster is two-thirds white. Up at Williams, its eighteen-member squad has only two black players, and we counted seven black faces amid the seventy-five in its football photograph.

But football and basketball are only two of many college sports. The rosters of the remaining teams, with the occasional exception of track, are overwhelmingly white. As new programs have been added—as with rowing at Ohio State—white students now top the recruiting lists. One need only look at sports like lacrosse, golf, and hockey to see that the players got their start at private and suburban schools. So when Colby introduced women's ice hockey, it was clear it wouldn't be filling its positions from the inner cities. In fact, almost everyone on its current team comes from exclusive—and expensive—schools like Tabor, Taft, and St. Paul's.

The upsurge in "white" sports is a partial explanation for why students from private schools have an admissions advantage at selective colleges. After all, few public high schools nurture their students in sports like ice hockey, golf, and crew. So though nationally private schools, including those with religious ties, account for only 10 percent of all high school graduates, they provide 40 percent of Stanford's admissions, along with 46 percent of Colby's and 45 percent of Yale's.

And there's another kind of diversity. With tennis, coaches have a penchant for overseas recruits. As we write, of Berkeley's nine women players, six are from abroad, including Germany, Hungary, and Australia. In a recent NCAA tennis tournament, forty-eight of the sixty-four male finalists were foreign nationals. As we saw, this was how Ohio State keeps women's rowing going. In a further twist, the imported players tend to be several years older, and come with more stamina and experience. Brooklyn's St. Francis College has a water polo team, but only three of its fifteen members started as regular students. The other twelve were invited, sight unseen, from Israel, Hungary, and Serbia, given student visas, and automatic admission. We'll grant that this adds to the diversity of the college. Still, overseas recruiting is yet another consequence of intercollegiate competition; colleges and coaches want to come in first, even if they have to go to Munich and Melbourne to assemble winning teams. As a result, American students sit by and watch while foreign recruits carry the name of their college.

Myth: Expanding women's sports imperils men's programs.
Reality: Here the poster victim is men's wrestling. Between 1982 and 2008, the number of schools sponsoring this very male sport dropped from 363 to 227. The reason most commonly given is that Title IX demands parity of men's and women's participation in athletic programs, or at the least strong efforts toward that goal. Since historically most teams were for men, to even up the numbers colleges had to show a substantial increase in women's programs.

And they have. In 1982, only 80 colleges sponsored women's soccer teams; now 956 do. Colby not only installed ice hockey for women, it also added women's teams for golf, lacrosse, crew, squash, plus two kinds of skiing. Even so, at most schools, budgets are limited, so decisions were made that some men's sports would have to go. Wrestling was on a lot of hit lists. "The number of collegiate wrestling teams lost to Title IX compliance is staggering," the novelist John Irving exclaimed in the *New York Times*. He was right; or at least partly so. As we've seen, there are now 136 fewer wrestling programs, a drop of over a third. Since fully 149 swimming teams for women have been started, it's tempting to assume that their arrival had some causal connection to the demise of those 136 wrestling teams.

Since we're not supporters of any varsity sports and believe that the only good college sports are club teams with volunteer coaches, we don't view adding teams for either gender as a cause for celebration. Still, it's best to keep the facts straight. Clearly, women have become a distinctive presence on fields and courts and rinks. As the table on page 165 shows, they now field almost twice as many teams as in 1982, when records were first kept.

At that time, some argued that women wouldn't be interested in demanding sports. Yet in just over a quarter-century, 103,845 new women signed up for 4,704 new teams. Indeed, all colleges together now have more women's programs: 9,469 against 8,448 for men.

The table also tells a lesser-known story: taken together, men's teams and their participants have *not* been losing ground. Granted, there are 1,604 fewer wrestlers. But that loss is well outweighed by 70,461 *new* men who have joined teams since 1982, particularly football. We confess that when we began our study, we weren't aware that 132 schools have added this costly sport, with 23,462 more men playing. Or at least warming benches. Since 1982, the average size of football rosters has grown from 82 to 102 players. So if the current midpoint is near 102, it must mean many are a lot higher. MIT has only 58 on its squad, and Williams makes do with 75. But the University of Texas bench has 116, and the University of Tennessee feels it needs 137, which equals the total rosters of seven of its women's teams.

Coaches demand numbers like these because football has become so hyper-specialized that each player is prepared for a detailed task. This has redefined the sport so that even a small school like Birmingham Southern, which enrolls only 564 men, puts 122 of them on its football squad. We cite these numbers since they relate to the issue we raised earlier, the disappearance of 1,604 wrestlers. They and their teams could easily have been saved had their own colleges refrained from inflating their football rosters. So if a few men's athletic programs have been discarded, it's a *mano a mano* problem.

Myth: Profits from well-attended sports help pay for other teams.
Reality: It's true that some teams turn a profit. But it's not easy to say how many, because we must rely on the creative accountings that colleges submit to the NCAA and the U.S. Department

TEAMS AND PLAYERS: GAINS AND LOSSES

MEN'S TEAMS

1982				2008	
TEAMS	PLAYERS			TEAMS	PLAYERS
6,746	167,006	All Teams		8,341	233,830
497	40,773	Football		625	62,459
442	17.229	Baseball		897	29,486
138	4,193	Lacrosse		226	3,353
363	7,918	Wrestling		229	6,227

WOMEN'S TEAMS

1982				2008	
TEAMS	PLAYERS			TEAMS	PLAYERS
4,765	74,106	All Teams		9,469	178,084
80	1,855	Soccer		956	22,682
436	7,841	Softball		950	17,154
125	1,060	Golf		516	4,096
179	2,063	Gymnastics		85	1,430

of Education. We'll do the best we can with this reporting; after all, you have to start somewhere. In our reading, of the 1,013 men's basketball teams, fewer than fifty end up with black ink. With football, which is much more expensive but has bigger attendance, of the 618 teams, at most, forty collect more than they spend. But in both sports, the margins can be razor-thin.

Duke is a major basketball power, regularly filling all its seats. In a recent year, it took in $15,903,075 but paid out $15,047,983, leaving an ostensible profit of $855,092 to help Duke's twenty-two other sports. Texas Tech football reported revenues of $18,710,471 and $18,530,666 in expenses, netting $187,805 for its fourteen other teams.

Women's basketball at the University of Tennessee is one of the nation's top programs and is constantly in the news. Its coach, Pat Summitt, is a media celebrity, and recently won a contract that will net her $1.3 million a year. This might make a kind of sense if her operation were profitable. But big-time basketball is costly, with $131,913 expended annually on each Lady Vol. (Tennessee's male swimmers make do with $4,105 each.) As a result, it ends up with a deficit. So we're not sure what justifies her seven-figure payout—except perhaps a sense that if they are over-paying male coaches, the new equality demands something like parity.

If, at the very most, a hundred teams make money, at best only a dozen athletic departments cover their own costs, or do a little better. Sometimes, at their own discretion, they share their largess. In a recent affluent year, Ohio State's sports programs gave $5 million to help renovate the library, and the University of Florida's athletic officials donated $6 million toward academic scholarships. Each year, about $600,000 from sales of Texas athletic paraphernalia goes to the university's president for his discretionary fund. And that's essentially it. There's not a single college or university that can count on a revenue stream from their varsity teams. Even when millions come in—Texas revenues recently exceeded $100 million—ways are found to use them within the athletics complex (a field house always needs refurbishing). Nor do annual balance sheets tell the whole story. Princeton says it spends $1,801,579 annually on its football squad. But just a year or so ago, it opened a $45 million stadium, which the team will use at most six times a year. Nor are we sure what other uses the college will find for this 27,773-seat arena. We leave it to accountants to tell us how much of that structure's cost should be added to each year's football budget.

Myth: *Mens Sana in Corpore Sano*
Reality: Let's listen to Estep Nagy, a Yale alumnus writing the *New York Review of Books* in response to an article that Andrew wrote. This former Eli describes what he got from stroking on the college crew:

> Day after day, month after month, year after year, to compete at these levels requires not only major sacrifices, but also a toughness, fortitude, and sense of purpose that, I would argue, is an essential part of a meaningful education.

Well put. And we'll accept that the fortitude and sense of purpose he describes was related to varsity competition. He and his fellow oarsmen weren't enduring all those grueling hours on the Quinnipiac just to burnish their biceps. They had a nobler reason: it was to get in shape to beat Harvard, and perhaps meet and defeat Oxford or Cambridge.

For our own part, we'll grant that intramural softball can't summon this depth of dedication. So is the inference that every undergraduate should spend time on a varsity team? Those who don't, we seem to be hearing, are missing an integral part of the college experience.

Of course, we favor physical activity. (Do we really have to say this?) In our sedentary era, we spend too much of our lives on sofas and seats; we drive when we should walk, and eat more than what we need. That said, we'll ask a naïve question: are colleges obliged to minister to students' bodies as well as their minds? True, something akin to gym is required in most high schools, but they make many things compulsory that colleges do not. Still, most people would say that a even a no-frills college might have a swimming pool, perhaps a running track, space for basketball, maybe some tennis courts. So allow us again to at least ask the question: *Why?* How do such amenities contribute to the pursuit we have been calling higher education?

Our view throughout this book has been that every non-educational appendage should be made to defend its existence, from the ground up and without the benefit of any doubt. We would apply this stricture to art museums, career counseling, and chaplain's offices. We'd ask the same of swimming pools, tennis teams, and golf matches against other colleges. If it's more than minimal facilities, are they really necessary?

But back to Estep Nagy's argument about crew and the benefits from those days and months of training aimed at defeating rival colleges. Here's our response. According to the NCAA, a typical men's rowing team has twenty-eight members, and a year's cost comes to $785,400. If Yale's tab is much like this, it is laying out $28,050 annually for each rower, which comes to $112,200 for four years of stroking a shell. Even acknowledging that lessons are learned in fortitude, we feel compelled to conclude that crew is a luxury in which not even Yale should be indulging.

Reasonable people can differ on what's essential to an undergraduate education. We're sure someone will vote for fraternities and homecoming bonfires. Our list would start with writing an archaeology thesis, staging a production of *Othello*, and launching a literary magazine. In fact, relatively few undergraduates end up wearing a varsity uniform. By our count, only 6 percent of college men and 3.6 percent of college women spend time on any kind of team. At the University of Illinois, a fairly typical state school, it's only 2 percent of the undergraduate body.

There's another problem about the intercollegiate impetus. Well over half the sponsored sports are those that graduates are unlikely to ever play again. That's clearly so for wrestling and water polo, almost certainly for lacrosse, ice hockey, and probably for gymnastics and synchronized swimming. At least the habit of reading, which can be reinforced at college, has a long afterlife.

Sound minds in sound bodies—how could one object? So here's another cause for misgiving, at least with how the athletic life is being construed. The near-professional performance expected of college players takes a toll. Fully half of the University of Michigan's football squad require surgery in a typical year. As a result, its medical school has opened an orthopedic clinic in the sports complex. Nor is the cost wholly physical. Stanford's softball 2009 schedule ran for fifteen weeks, entailing fifty-eight games, half of them away. That's right: basically four games a week, including traveling to states like Massachusetts, Texas, and Arizona. When do those softballers attend class? We leave to your imagination how well they can keep up with their coursework, say, when they are slotted to play on February 8, 9, 10, 13, 15, 16, and 17. A Stanford professor told us she regularly gets letters from the athletics department, listing students who won't be in class on playing days. "While they don't request undue consideration, the message is implicit," she said. "They tread a fine line." Much can be said for softball. The young women who play it seem to enjoy it, and it's a game you can carry into middle age. Still, indulge us a question: why a need for 58 games in a single semester?

Myth: Memorable experiences, meeting new people.
Reality: We can agree that traveling to play at other colleges is an experience non-athletes don't ordinarily have. (But let's not forget the debating team.) There's the piling into a bus, a van, or a plane, and on arrival having to adjust to an unfamiliar pool or rink or court. Once more, allow us a naïve question. Since there are usually several colleges within, say, a 100-mile radius, why is it necessary to travel great distances for the away experience?

During the 2009 season, here are some of the schools that jour-
neyed to Palo Alto to play softball against Stanford: Notre Dame
(1,921 miles); Western Kentucky (1,956 miles); Princeton (2,553
miles); University of Vermont (2,533 miles). Princeton sent its track
teams to race in China (7,367 miles), which was undoubtedly a
memorable experience. Still, the tab came to $200,000, which
didn't raise eyebrows when money was readily available. We'll
agree athletes encounter new people when visiting other campuses, whether from Western Kentucky or Nanjing University.
But these meetings are usually ephemeral, perhaps a half hour
between the final whistle and boarding a bus. Nor are we sure
what interactions take place after 100-man squads from Penn
State and Ohio State file off to their separate locker rooms.

Myth: Varsity sports inspire loyalty and bolster donations.
Reality: The first fact of athletic life is that to the extent that college teams inspire loyalty and donations, it is only when they win.
Students and alumni and donors don't show much sympathy for
programs that keep on losing. Sure, spectators occasionally cheer
on an underdog. But after a while, as attendance figures show,
most just stop showing up. A Dartmouth student succinctly told
us why there are so many empty seats at its football games: "They
don't win enough." So it's not enough to sponsor an array of
teams. They have to register winning records over successive
seasons. Nor do such programs emerge spontaneously. They are
a result of expensive investments in equipment, coaches, and
recruiting.

Yet the myth persists that athletics pay off. A professor we
know at Emory, one of the few major universities without football, recently heard a development officer arguing for starting a
program because, he claimed, "it increases alumni donations tremendously." From what we can see, the only thing it would do
would be to build up this fund-raiser's CV; he'd forever be known

as "the man who brought football to Emory." That's how reputations are made in academe.

Sometimes, a Division II or III school will be urged to upgrade, so it will meet more newsworthy opponents. As we hear with investing generally, you must spend money to make money. The University of Texas branch in San Antonio was told it would need $14 million per year in new money to break into Division I-A. To start, more would be needed for travel ($450,000), recruiting ($120,000), and remitting tuitions and room and board ($2 million) if it wanted to sign up more competitive players. Not to mention academic training rooms, tutoring, and broadcasting booths. Since donors weren't lining up, the bulk of the new costs would fall on its undergraduates, each of whom was slated to pay a $500 fee to support the venture.

When the powers-that-be at the Binghamton branch of the State University of New York decided to upgrade their basketball team to NCAA Division I, they turned their school into the poster-child of all that can go wrong in the quest for athletic glory. The aggressive recruitment of players resulted in a near crime wave: drug dealing, shoplifting, credit card theft. One team member was arrested for stealing condoms from the local Wal-Mart; he later tried to get a coach to pay his fine.

Athletes with questionable academic records were admitted and then sent for "independent studies" with a professor having a track record as a sports fan. Big and little corruptions abounded. A player was given transfer credit for "Bowling I" and "Theories of Softball." (We'd love sit in on those courses.) And when an adjunct blew the whistle on how players were being coddled, she found herself jobless. Binghamton's chancellor was questioned about these and other misdemeanors; she said it was the result of an "experiment" in diversity.

This has happened at other schools before. Yet, the myth still holds that big-time sports are the surest fix for a university's sagging public profile. When Claudia visited Mississippi Valley State University, a mostly black college in the still impoverished Delta, she asked some of its academic leaders what was on their wish list for improving the school. And it certainly could use some help: it ranks below most of its peers, not least because only 35 percent of its students graduate and its faculty budget merely allows for seventeen full professors. But at the top of one official's list was a new football stadium, which he felt would upgrade the school's reputation and draw more students.

Since this hope is so often voiced, economists have looked for evidence to back it. The research we've reviewed has found that donations do tend to rise—by about 7 percent—if a school attains a football bowl slot or basketball's Final Four play-offs. So we see that some donors can be turned on by winners. Needless to say, the vast majority of teams never get nearly that far, including those that invest heavily in hope of reaching those summits.

So it's best not to rely on athletics as a financial magnet. But there's more. Alumni and others who write checks tend to earmark their money for supporting athletic programs. The University of Missouri's Tiger Club is fairly typical. It raised nearly $7 million in a recent year to pay for players' room and board, along with "academic counselors, tutors, and career development." However, this aid is only available to team members. So at Missouri, athletes now get proportionately more assistance than students admitted for their academic promise.

We did a simple exercise to see if sponsoring football bolsters alumni support. Colleges tell *U.S. News & World Report* how many of their graduates gave money in the previous year. The box on the next page lists twelve schools, half that have football and half that never did or have ended their programs. (All are private institutions, to keep comparisons consistent.) We merely remark that if sponsoring football spurs donations at some schools—although we're not convinced it's a key factor— alumni loyalty seems similar at schools that don't have that

BLOCKING, TACKLING, AND GIVING

Percentage of Alumni Who Contribute

COLLEGES WITH FOOTBALL		COLLEGES WITHOUT FOOTBALL	
Bates College	43%	Haverford College	47%
Hamilton College	48%	Swarthmore College	48%
Rice University	34%	Emory University	37%
Vanderbilt University	24%	Brandeis University	32%
Syracuse University	18%	Marquette	18%
Seton Hall	9%	New York University	11%

sport.

Indeed, it seems to us there's a negative correlation between the generosity of gifts and investing in athletics. The *Chronicle of Higher Education* listed all gifts of $100 million or more given to colleges and universities between 2000 and 2008. Of the forty-five recipient institutions, only three had leading football programs (University of Texas, Southern California, Berkeley). Even more don't sponsor football (Emory, NYU, Cal Tech, Yeshiva, University of the Pacific). And some that do can hardly be called athletic powers (Tufts, Claremont McKenna, Johns Hopkins, University of Chicago).

At the Cooper Union for the Arts and Sciences, they do athletics differently. This genuinely selective New York City arts and engineering college offers every student it admits a full-tuition scholarship. As a result, there's little left in the budget for the luxuries that have become routine at so many other schools. If colleges want to sponsor athletic programs, we propose Cooper Union as a model. It has fifteen sports, including volleyball, basketball, soccer, and tennis. Athletics play no part in admissions decisions. It's only after students begin their freshman year that they can pick a team, and then only for fun. The school's annual sports budget totals about $20,000 annually, or $20 per student. Therefore, team members practice in a gym rented from a nearby church and they travel to games on public transportation.

Steve Baker, Cooper Union's dean of student services and the head of the program, expects his athletes to study fifty hours a week. If they want to chase a ball, it's up to them to find the time and place. The school's big basketball star gets up at six in the morning to practice at a public park. Baker's calling card says it all: *No Gym, No Courts, No Fields, No Pool, No Horses, No Time, No Excuses.* Still, his teams don't do badly. A few years ago, one won in the Hudson Valley women's tennis finals. As Baker once put it, "Most teams we play are bigger than us, spend more time practicing than we do and they actually expect to win the game. All we're out there doing is learning and having fun."

· 10 ·

STUDENT BODIES

On a stroll around almost any campus, here are some things that will catch your eye. First, if you had been a student yourself some years ago, you'll note fewer Caucasian faces than in your time. Also, you will see more black and Hispanic students, although at more selective schools they may be outnumbered by their Asian classmates. And the odds are strong that you'll encounter more women than men. Finally, as you pass by the parking lots, make a count of late-model vehicles, since that's a good index of student affluence.

This chapter will offer information about who is attending college and who isn't, about efforts to expand enrollments, and who benefits from the rules and rituals of the admissions process. Here as elsewhere, higher education isn't an abstraction. It is about the young people for whom college—or its lack—will be a turning point in their lives. The postmodernists, of whom we are generally not very fond, claim that everything is a "social construct," meaning that matters of race, gender, and class are human contrivances. When it comes to college admissions, they are most certainly right—as we shall see.

CHANGING COMPLEXIONS

Starting in the 1960s, elite colleges decided that they wanted a more visible black and Hispanic presence. Hence their use of affirmative action, which has been an object of controversy, from domestic dinner tables to pleadings before the Supreme Court.

Entire books have been devoted to this topic, so we'll confine ourselves to a few observations. One is that the *affirmative* part means just that. Colleges do not simply wait for applications to come in. Rather, they take active steps to attract candidates of the desired race or ethnicity. It should be added that such steps are still legal for private institutions, which are not as strictly bound by the "equal protection" provision of the Constitution. So private Smith College can refuse to open applications from men. Brigham Young can favor adherents of the Latter-day Saints by charging them less for tuition. Or MIT can admit women with lower mathematics scores to secure a better gender balance. In the same vein, private colleges like Dartmouth and Duke can use special admissions criteria for the black and Hispanic applicants they want. However, public universities no longer have that leeway. Due to state laws, judicial decisions, and popular referendums, they are not allowed to base admissions on attributes people inherently have, like their complexion or place of birth or gender.

The professors and presidents at the most sought-after colleges tend to be politically liberal. So they try to increase the black and Hispanic representations on their campus and have made extra efforts to find such students and provide the funding they may need. At most recent count, 15 percent of Harvard's students are from these two groups, as are 17 percent at Duke, and 22 percent at Stanford. What this must mean is that some white and Asian applicants with good records are being rejected in order to fill affirmative action places. In 1980, white students at Harvard made up 86 percent of its undergraduates; they are now down to 58 percent. At Duke, their share has dropped from 92 percent to 64 percent.

When two white applicants contested affirmative action at the University of Michigan, they claimed that places that should have been theirs were given to less qualified candidates. Undoubtedly, some white applicants who have been rejected by Duke and Harvard may also feel this way.

White students who feel aggrieved tend to be at the bottom of the white list. *White list?* Surely, admissions deans will insist, there's no such thing. But we wonder. We recall hearing from Tom Parker, who guards the gate at Amherst College, saying that his mission is not so much to pass judgment on individuals but rather to "build a class." So he is looking for a freshman intake that includes a mix of chess champions, lacrosse stars, and cello players. In reviewing the makeup of a possible class, the problem could arise that it looks "too white." Were that the case, some Caucasians will have to be dropped; and it seems clear that they will come, yes, from the bottom of the white list.

Affirmative action—the great bugaboo of conservatives, at least as it applies to race—is in fact only operative at selective colleges that have the resources to search for and offer financial support to the students they want. Many, indeed most, black and Hispanic applicants need such aid if they are to accept an offer from a school like Williams, which has a $39,490 tuition tab. Williams has lifted these two groups to 19 percent of its students by a generous use of scholarship funds—or at least they did that until the recent economic downturn. (As this book goes to press, there are indications that Williams is cutting back on financial aid.) Other colleges would have liked to boast similar figures, but they lacked the wherewithal. Colby's black and Hispanic total is 5 percent. Coe College in Iowa can manage only 4 percent, and Hanover in Indiana must settle for 2 percent.

The most recent counts show that the overwhelming majority of the 146,653 black students who received a bachelor's degree in 2008, as well as their 114,936 Hispanic classmates, did not gain their places from affirmative action preferences. For one thing, about a fifth of black graduates come from colleges that were originally created for their race. And most of the rest are at less selective public colleges, which in any event cannot readily use race-based preferences.

For the traditional minorities—blacks and Hispanics—the problem has not so much been admission to four-year colleges. Rather, it has been finishing the four years and obtaining the preparation that will usher them into graduate school and professional careers. Currently, black freshmen are 63 percent as likely to graduate as their white peers; for Hispanics, it's 59 percent. In particular, neither group has been able to enter the hard sciences and engineering in anything like significant numbers. In the 1960s, fewer than 1 percent of the PhDs in what the technocrats call STEM (science, technology, engineering, mathematics) were awarded to African Americans. By 2008, after ostensible efforts to open opportunities, their share had inched up to 2.1 percent.

Enter Freeman Hrabowski III, a mathematician and statistician who has been a top administrator at the University of Maryland's branch at Baltimore County since 1982. As a twelve-year-old, he was a child leader in Martin Luther King Jr.'s demonstrations against segregation in Birmingham, Alabama. Later, as an educator, Hrabowski used his influence to, as he put it, "increase the number of Americans, particularly African Americans who excel in science and engineering." In 1988, with seed money from two Baltimore philanthropists, Jane and Robert Meyerhoff, he began scouting bright black students throughout the state, the sort who might otherwise be recruited by top private schools. What he offered was scholarship, "bridge" classes to prepare them for intense college science studies, and one-on-one tutoring—all in a college within a college where they would be nurtured and encouraged.

For two decades, the Meyerhoffs and Hrabowski have offered affirmative action, with an open emphasis on race. Hrabowski summarized the project's progress for us: "We have gone from the first nineteen Meyerhoff Scholars who enrolled in the program in its initial year, 1989, to graduating approximately six hundred Meyerhoff students to date with bachelor's degrees in science and engineering. Of this group, 85 percent have gone on for their master's, doctorates, as well as combined MD-PhD programs."

The achievements of the Meyerhoff scholars are a big lesson to those who emphasize the obstacles facing women and minorities in certain areas of study. What's required is an interface of wish and will. Complexions on campuses are changing. With leadership, the spectrum can be even more representative. At this juncture, it's proper to focus on the race and gender and upbringing of students, because they delineate obstacles that have to be overcome. This nation has always stood for equity and opportunity—our colleges should be in the forefront of attaining those goals.

THE ASIAN ARRIVAL

Many of the places whites once held are now being filled by students of Asian origin. Since 1980, their share of all bachelor's degrees has more than tripled, from 2 percent to almost 7 percent. At first reading, these percentages may seem fairly small, but the impact at the most selective colleges is large. Here's one way to tell the story: in 1980 at both Harvard and Penn there were only five Asian students on their campuses for every one hundred whites. By 2009, perhaps coincidentally, the ratio at both was nearing thirty per one hundred. In 1980, MIT had only seven Asians for each hundred whites; 2009 found eighty per one hundred, over a tenfold increase.

True, during this period, the total white portion of the population was declining. Nevertheless, the number able to afford selective schools had actually increased, as had the pool with college-educated parents. By these measures, white applicants should have been able to maintain a competitive edge. Yet Asians were displacing them, and it was on academic merit, not through affirmative action. More of them had better grades, as well as higher scores on the tests that white psychologists had invented. In every income bracket, Asian students surpassed whites. Indeed, on the mathematics and writing portions of the SAT, Asian women outscore white men. We hear a great deal about the strenuous preparation of white applicants, including coaching for the SAT and college essays. Yet these efforts apparently don't match the dedication of their Asian classmates, who have a special motivation. Among our own Asian students, we've observed that honoring their parents is part of what impels them to excel; anything less than a full A is taken as disgrace.

There's more to affirmative action, although it's not usually described by those words. White applicants who are not strong on the academic side have other roads to admission. One way around so-so grades and scores is to have parents who attended the college. The best study we've seen found that legacy offspring have a 24 percent greater chance of acceptance than the general run of applicants, which doesn't help Asians, since as we noted earlier, few have alumni parents. Another white route is to be flagged for sports like ice hockey and lacrosse or golf and tennis, which are most commonly played in suburban and private schools. The applicants that coaches really want have a 48 percent edge over more sedentary applicants. Tom Parker of Amherst told us how coaches are constantly in his office, arguing for students flagged as a hockey goalie or a lacrosse midfielder. These applicants are almost always Caucasian.

Another study also parsed the records of Asian applicants at highly selective schools. In actual fact, 24 percent of them were admitted. But had a "color-blind" method been used, 32 percent would have been given places. The short answer is that these colleges impose quotas due to fears that they may appear "too Asian," just as in earlier decades schools were anxious about becoming "too Jewish."

Public colleges now face greater scrutiny, and so have less leeway with skewed admissions. Even Texas A&M has abolished legacy preferences. California's university system emphasizes academic records, partly due to a desire for equity, but also because most of their campuses have so many applicants that they can't go deeply into the folders. Due to the stress on grades and scores, Asians now outnumber Caucasians at the University of California's Berkeley, Los Angeles, San Diego, and Irvine branches. True, California has a large Asian population. Even so, whites still outnumber them by a factor of four in the state's college-age cohort. The simple fact is that whites, even in better-off families, aren't doing as well in California's high schools. A wag told us that UCLA is now said to stand for "Unhappy Caucasians Lost among Asians."

MORE WOMEN, FEWER MEN

Let's return to that campus stroll. At a typical four-year college, you'll count 127 women for every 100 men. By the time the graduation rolls around, there will be 133 women for each 100 men receiving degrees. This holds across a spectrum. For example, North Carolina's Elon University is now 59 percent female, and New York University's ratio is 61 percent. Higher education used to be mainly a male preserve. Back in 1955, women accounted for only 38 percent of all college places. The genders drew equal in 1980, but women kept on enrolling. The most recent tabulations showed they receive slightly over 57 percent of the bachelor's degrees.

The reasons are not hard to find. In high school, more girls sign up for college-track courses, where they achieve higher grades. Teachers attest they are likely to complete assignments and pay attention in class. The fruits of 1970s feminism have changed attitudes and opened most areas of study to women. Whether or not they identify with that movement, young women now benefit from its achievements by aspiring to careers, accompanied by a surer sense of themselves. It follows that more women are applying and are better qualified for admission.

From a nationwide standpoint, men don't have trouble being accepted. But there are fewer places for them now in the much coveted colleges that were once all male and opted to become coeducational. When they began admitting women, these schools expanded their enrollments, but not hugely. The result was that fewer men were admitted. In 1970, prior to coeducation, all of Dartmouth's 3,270 places were, obviously, taken by men. But by 2009, it had room for only 1,982 men on its rolls. This means there will be 1,208 fewer men able to go through life saying they had been at Dartmouth. Similarly, Yale now has 2,019 fewer men than it did a generation ago. The earlier Harvard was only nominally coeducational, allowing merely a fifth of its seats to Radcliffe women. But women are now close to half of Harvard's rolls, which also reduces the male pool. Of course, these missing men won't be stocking shelves at Costco—Lehigh and Lewis & Clark will be pleased to take them. Even so, these fallback schools don't have the same cachet, and for many parents and students, that's what really counts. There's a pleasant backstory to how these Ivy schools became coed. At all of them, the faculties pressed for admitting women. Some professors found it stultifying to teach only men; others said we live in a two-gender world, and campuses should reflect that reality. Trustees tended to be neutral. The big worry was the alumni, who cherished memories of manly days at Dartmouth, Yale, and Princeton. Yet alumni opposition never materialized; in fact, they hardly raised a peep. An Amherst professor told us why: "Most of our graduates also had daughters. And they wanted them to be able to go where they did."

The preponderance of women has several other twists. Without saying so directly, most colleges would like to push the clock back to a fifty-fifty balance. As one dean quipped, "We're called William and Mary, not Mary and Mary." The imbalance puts many women in a bind. For social reasons, some would like equal gender numbers, if not a preponderance of men. At the same time, they want to get into their chosen schools, and bringing in more men would diminish their chances. As a partial step, some schools deploy a variant of affirmative action to let in less-qualified men. Figures we've seen for 2007 showed that Brown admitted 16 percent of its male applicants, but only 13 percent of the women. Yale and Williams had similar gender gaps. Private institutions can do this legally; while as we've noted, public colleges face constitutional constraints. Thus federal courts overturned a University of Georgia attempt to give extra admissions points to men. Still, to make their campuses more attractive to men, 121 schools have added football to their athletic programs since 1982.

There's also a class dimension to the sexual imbalance. The best information we have comes from the Educational Testing Service, which asks college applicants about their family's income. We found it revealing that in lower-income homes, women are more likely to make it to college. This now occurs in all ethnic groups, including Asians and Hispanics, who historically haven't always encouraged their daughters. Stated another way, men are more likely to continue into higher education if they have well-off parents, whereas more women are doing it on their own.

In a world where women have ascended from 38 percent of college graduates to over 57 percent, things will never be the same, whether it's the texture of marriages, professional employment, or simply how people view themselves. The same stricture applies to the men's decline from 62 percent to 43 percent. Where are the missing men? The most obvious answer is that many of college age are in the military and prison, particularly among minority groups and the poor. As we've just seen, more women come to college from lower-income homes, which attests to a stamina and dedication not always evident in their brothers and boyfriends.

But even in well-off families, fewer young men are continuing their education. A Brookings Institution study has a telling statistic. It found that close to half—47 percent—of children who were raised in the top economic quintile do not end up with bachelor's degrees. This is perplexing. After all, well-off parents are supposed to be able to ensure advantages for their offspring. Our own findings suggest that they are mostly sons who won't be mirroring the successes of their fathers. What we're ultimately seeing is that the justification for discrimination against young women in higher education, rampant since its earliest days, has lost its last shards of authority. Once college admissions became, more or less, a question of merit, women excelled. One of the authors of this book remembers how in her freshman English composition class, circa 1962, she had to read an essay with the title "Why Bother Educating Girls?" With the academic triumphs of female undergraduates, we can see how many of our old ideas about who should study and who shouldn't were "socially constructed."

"Life isn't fair," John F. Kennedy once said. Indeed, he knew this to be so, since he began life with a host of advantages. So we will simply add that higher education isn't fair, either. At this point, two-thirds of young Americans will not be attending college or will drop out if they do. We may like to style ourselves as a middle-class nation, but most young people don't have the kind of parental backstop that can help to make four full years of college possible. Our opinion on this matter is straightforward. Just as in an earlier century we decided that every American should finish high school, we should now make completing college this century's goal.

RICHER AND POORER

Whereas most people want to feel that learning can and should be pursued as an end in itself, they also see higher education as a vehicle for mobility. It may even be argued that these goals are not opposed: in theory, an improved intellect should enhance your worth in the marketplace. Regarding upward movement, much attention is given to students who are the first in their family to go to college. And rightly so. An equitable society must open opportunities for those who start with fewer advantages. Here too the best information we have comes from an Educational Testing Service survey of high school seniors who plan to go to college. Each was asked about his or her parent who had the most education. Using these figures to make some further calculations, we concluded that students with college-educated parents stand a five times better chance of getting a degree than those from non-college homes. If one of our goals for higher education is to encourage mobility, we're not doing a very good job.

As it happens, money can provide an extra edge in the application process. Take the "personal essay," which most colleges now require. How to submit one that will stand out from the rest in a towering pile? An answer is to write out a draft and send it with $595 to a business enterprise called Merlyn's Pen. Their staff will help you recast it so that admissions officers will, as Merlyn's website has attested, "put down their coffee and take notice." Their fee includes telephone consultations with a Merlyn "mentor" who, they tell you, will help you find your "voice." At Merlyn, they see nothing untoward about having a professional adult suggest touches for a paper to which students will append their names.

Admissions officers tend to take this as a fact of life. Jonathan Burdick at the University of Rochester told us he can detect "obvious interference." Still, we suspect Merlyn-type mentors are adept at retaining enough teenage touches to add authenticity to the submission. Burdick adds that even when doing course assignments while at college, he senses "half the students sitting at their computer are still getting someone's help with an essay."

Then there's the Scholastic Assessment Test, the ubiquitous SAT, whose scores are usually the first items at which schools look (although at Brown University, the word *legacy* goes at the top of the folder). A typical Kaplan SAT class—twelve sessions in all—will set you back $1,000. For that sum, Kaplan offers twelve Sunday classes, which explain how to outfox multiple-choice questions and when guessing will pay off. For $9,500, the Princeton Review, Kaplan's rival, will provide twenty-five at-home meetings with your own tutor. The market has become nationwide. The $9,500 fee we cited was in reply to an inquiry we made from Fort Smith, Arkansas. Test preparation has become a $1 billion industry. Indeed, Kaplan was purchased by the *Washington Post* and has become one of its principal profit centers. For those with deeper pockets, there is "Application Boot Camp," which advertises in Princeton's alumni magazine, and provides more details on an elaborate website. At its low end, it offers a four-day session, presided over by a former Dartmouth admissions officer. Advice is given on making the most of high school activities, plus practice in how to conduct yourself in interviews with alumni or on campus visits. The four-day cost—hold your breath—is $14,000, which doesn't include hotel stays or breakfasts and dinners. Its website claims its pupils have "gotten YES letters" from Yale, Harvard, Stanford, and most of the others on the hardest-to-crack list. Also included are letters from grateful students, saying they couldn't have made it without Boot Camp. ("You have taken away a ton of my stress and provided me with valuable advice. I cannot express how relieved, overjoyed, and honored I am to be accepted to Amherst College.")

But there's more. For upward of $40,000, Boot Camp staff members Michelle and Mimi offer an inclusive "consulting package." As we read it, they become surrogate parents, constantly on the phone with help and hints, including e-mail tips and prompts, throughout the entire admissions season. They say that even the best high school college advisors can't provide such attention. To strengthen this pitch, they claim that their "biggest client base" contains pupils from already-privileged Andover, Exeter, and St. Paul's. True, not all of their clients reach Olympus. So Boot Camp should get points for honesty, since they admit that some of their clients end up at less selective schools like Macalester College and the University of Denver.

College fund-raising appeals like to say that much of the money they receive goes into scholarships, enabling students from modest backgrounds to attend expensive colleges. Is this truly the case? The best measure of the percentage of lower-income students on campus is how many are receiving federal Pell grants, which are usually reserved for families with incomes under $45,000. Reports we've seen show Pell percentages at Northwestern, Vanderbilt, and Johns Hopkins to be under 10 percent, as they are at colleges like Middlebury, Colby, and Davidson. Even after much publicized recruiting for applicants from modest homes, Pell-tier students at Princeton and Harvard make up less than 7 percent of their undergraduate bodies. High-status public universities do slightly better, but not by much. Madison and Ann Arbor manage about 12 percent. But the University of Virginia, which each year looks more like a private school, has a Pell quotient of 7.5 percent. At the 42 most selective state campuses, 40 percent of the Class of 2009 came from homes with incomes over $100,000.

Colleges are aware that their charges are beyond the means of even middle-class Americans. As we've noted, they make much of how much they lay out for "scholarships" and "financial aid." Yet in fact they also devote a lot of their resources to assistance for higher-bracket applicants, especially if they have decent grades and scores. This has led at least a few parents to angle for discounted tuition, not to mention a certain amount of asset juggling. This isn't too difficult for self-employed professionals or where there has been a divorce. Parents may reply that tuition is purposely overpriced and they expect you to negotiate. Still, there's something unseemly about parents approaching higher education as if it were a rug purchase in the souk.

Harvard now offers discounted tuition to parents making as much as $180,000. A plan was crafted by Princeton in 2008, when $47,375 was needed for tuition, books, room, and meals. Families with incomes between $100,000 and $125,000 would be charged $19,675, which was under half the full tab. Other selective colleges have similar plans for what might be called the professional poverty line. An equally important bottom line is that colleges' cash flows depend on having a generous proportion of full payers. Figures provided by Stanford to the 2010 edition of the Princeton Review show that 57 percent of those it accepted needed no assistance whatever. At Yale, as we have pointed out, 58 percent could write checks for whole amount, as could 59 percent at Brown and 63 percent at Duke. These numbers help to explain all those late-model cars we mentioned in this chapter's opening page. Although colleges will never say it, they need a critical mass of full payers to balance their books. Might this mean that mildly affluent applicants—not just super-rich donors—have an extra edge when admission decisions are made? Simply to ask that question suggests the answer.

But we find it equally revealing that at elite colleges today, most alumni progeny are rejected. In the most recent counts we've seen, Harvard turns down 61 percent; at Swarthmore, it's 64 percent; and Princeton says sorry to almost two-thirds. Each year finds that more coveted places going to students with names like Singh and Chan and Kim.

Indeed, how student bodies get composed is a synthesis of the American way. In one stream, the affluent get an extra edge, since colleges need a contingent that doesn't ask for financial aid. In another, special consideration is given to applicants from unassuming backgrounds, often based on race or national origin. This attention reflects a sense of fairness, mingled with a bit of guilt. Then there's the merit stream. A physics whiz has to be given priority over a congenial candidate even if the latter's parents are dutiful alumni.

Of course, there isn't much consistency in this mix. Our colleges are part of the real world, reflecting the composition and aspirations of the larger society. But a visionary like Freeman Hrabowski doesn't simply accept the prevailing mosaic. He is making his college a social force in its own right, bringing in students who create a new configuration. Yet in one sense, the postmodernists have it right. Admissions offices are gripped by social constructs when they build their entering classes. At the end of the day, they implement these contrivances by what was once called "social engineering" as they attempt to reconcile ambiguous goals. Yet we often find ourselves asking, just to take one example, how far should Asians be cast as *Asian*? We've sat in on enough classes to observe that when Maliha Singh and Stanley Chan and Sylvia Kim contribute to class discussions it's not easy to detect what's identifiably "Asian" about their remarks on *Moby Dick* or Fermat's Theorem.

Our own goal is to make higher education's student body as universal—and so as varied and exciting—as possible. Each year, some four million new Americans are born, joined by others arriving here with immigrant parents. They all have minds and imaginations, and the potential to lead productive and distinctive lives. We're frequently tempted to suggest—close all the admissions offices and draw names from a bowl.

PART 4

FACING THE FUTURE

· 11 ·

VISITING THE FUTURE IN FLORIDA

For a glimpse into the future of higher education we paid a visit to Florida Gulf Coast University on the outskirts of Fort Myers. We chose it, in part, because it is new, having opened its doors in 1991. Indeed, it is a work in progress, unencumbered by traditions or an entrenched faculty. Currently 6,294 undergraduates are enrolled; almost all are residents of the state. Like most regional branches of state systems, Florida Gulf Coast doesn't try to be selective, and accepts three-quarters of its applicants. The faculty is committed and conscientious; the students we met are as bright as any we've met and as interested in learning.

The university's newness is pervasive, like a glistening coat of paint. Nor is it just the unblemished buildings. Almost all the professors have recently arrived in the state, just as its students are products of first-generation Florida. This also holds for the surroundings, where almost everything is recent. Since 1970, the population of greater Fort Myers has zoomed from 105,216 to 623,725. As the area has grown with no plan or rules, so the university is inventing itself. With nothing to build on or break away from, it has been awash in new ideas, in particular, placing technology at the center of teaching and learning.

Of course, this move isn't wholly new. An early effort was CBS's *Sunrise Semester* in the 1950s, which debuted with a New York University professor lecturing on Stendhal before a television camera. It was billed as a college experience without leaving your living room. Fast-forward to the present. MIT has taken the lead, having filmed almost 2,000 of its classes. This "courseware," as it is called, is now a widely used supplement. A professor in Kansas can project an MIT luminary on a screen to cover cutting-edge material.

John Gerassi often teaches in three classrooms simultaneously at the University of Hawaii. While he is physically with one group in Oahu, he has monitors beamed on others on the Maui and Kauai campuses. Via sound equipment, all three join in discussions. He says the distances dissolve as students become familiar with their other-island classmates. All of them see and hear Professor Gerassi, although for some it's not literally in the flesh. Needless to say, three at once brings a substantial cost-saving.

Professors in mathematics and the sciences now send students to what can be called techno-tutoring, eliminating sections once led by salaried assistants. Students call up programs, which guide them through formulas and equations, telling them to try again if they get a step wrong. (Home-schooling parents rely extensively on such software.) Many undergraduates say they find programmed explanations clearer than those given by graduate students. When software is deftly developed, it can provide better one-on-one mentoring than a lot of human teachers.

Which brings us to Florida Gulf Coast University. What caught our attention was that they had created a computer-based course called Understanding Visual and Performing Arts, a traditional liberal arts survey. Humanities 2510, its catalog designation, is compulsory and college-wide, and over 1,400 students were enrolled in the semester we visited. In many ways, the course is an apt test case for gauging technology's potential role in the liberal arts. After all, *Othello* isn't algebra, and *Starry Night* has no statistical solution. An exploration of the effectiveness of Humanities 2510 addresses important questions about what we expect colleges to be teaching and students to be learning.

But first, we'll take a moment to explain why Humanities 2510 turned to technology. It began using a traditional format, with sections of thirty-five to forty students, all of whom were taught by adjuncts hired from the Fort Myers area. But the course, as then organized, wasn't working. It was overly ambitious—trying to cover painting, photography, and sculpture, on through theater and dance. Unfortunately, none of the teaching adjuncts was familiar with all of the fields. The result: teachers focused on what they knew and students were left unprepared for the examinations. Its evaluations were atrocious. Still, Florida Gulf Coast wasn't ready to give up on its commitment to introduce all its undergraduates to the arts.

At that time it happened that a consulting group called the Center for Academic Transformation was telling colleges it knew of ways "to both improve student learning and reduce instructional costs." In higher education, as elsewhere, money is always an issue. Florida Gulf Coast must make do with only $5,081 per student for an academic year. (That's why the Humanities 2510 sections were taught by adjuncts rather than professors.) But of equal concern was that not much student learning was taking place. After an on-site review, the Center proffered this advice: eliminate the sections and tell the adjuncts they will no longer be needed. Indeed, it urged the faculty to "question the commonly held notion that the 'best' course is always a small one taught by a single instructor working alone."

The new Humanities 2510, which we observed in operation, has three basic features. First, there are no longer physical classes. Instead students sit at home or in their dorms, where they call up assignments, take tests, and prepare papers, all on their personal computers. Most of this can occur whenever students choose—2 a.m. is very popular—although tests and papers have due dates and times. In one sense, the course is "distance learning," now a commonly used phrase. But in Florida Gulf Coast's case, the students are on the campus; although in the future, others might take the course from far away.

Second, the recast Humanities 2510 continued to rely on a very low-tech device: a print-on-paper textbook. Given the many art forms, the coverage is necessarily brief. Dance is treated in thirteen pages; theater gets nineteen. And much of that space is filled with illustrations, which accounts for its $117 tab. More crucial, the book is the only real teacher, since there are no classroom discussions, or lectures with visual or audio aids. Of course, the 281 assigned pages must be mastered, since they are the only source of information and interpretations. So literally thousands of factoids—*intaglio, cantilever, ferroconcrete, cantata*—have to be memorized, as any could show up on a test.

Third, even if there are no on-campus instructors, human contact is made available. This is necessary; the 1,400 students write papers, all of which must be read. When we heard this, we saw it as a plus. Most colleges with ultra-large courses use only multiple-choice examinations, which are scanned and graded by computers. At Florida Gulf Coast, *preceptors,* as they are called, read all the students' papers and are available to answer questions. These exchanges are all by e-mail, with the corresponding parties never meeting in person. The reason, we learned, is that almost all the preceptors live elsewhere, even in distant states. They sign their full names to their e-mails, but do not append a photograph.

When we visited Fort Myers in the fall of 2009, the new incarnation of Understanding Visual and Performing Arts was in its seventh year. Several professors at the college oversee large sections to which the 1,400 students are assigned. Anne-Marie Bouche, an art historian who is one of them, told us that she is there to "manage the delivery of assignments" rather than be a "content provider." She said that perhaps ten of the three hundred students in her section have dropped by to see her personally, adding that they do so only when they are unhappy with grades or have deadline problems. "I don't believe I have ever had an inquiry about the substance of the course," says Morgan Paine, a faculty colleague who also has several hundred students on his list; he gets a substantive question "only once or twice a semester." Since his field is studio art, if it's about opera, he calls a friend in the music department.

For the first four weeks, the students are expected to read assigned chapters and take multiple-choice tests that arrive on the screens of their home computer. We've reproduced some questions on the next page. On these, they get immediate feedback: the computer flashes their grade almost the instant they've finished. In the fourth week, they receive an e-mail from a preceptor, who will be their continuing human contact in the class. As we've noted, all interchanges are by e-mail. Telephone calls are not allowed, so you never hear a voice.

We asked about those unseen preceptors. Their basic qualification is a bachelor's degree, with any field sufficing. Their own training for their role in the course was via online manuals. No need is seen to bring them to the campus for workshops where they might meet one another and share experiences. One preceptor we met had been a high school teacher and is now employed as an office manager and is pursuing an MBA. She is responsible for the work of 90 students. For this, she is paid $25 per head, or $2,250, for about twelve weeks' work, which she does mainly in the evenings. She said she knew of someone who had 300 students, but for her, it was a full-time job. The preceptors are not expected to be versed in all the subjects covered in the course, or even one of them. We asked her what she would do if a student asked her to elucidate something the textbook said about, say,

HUMANITIES 2510
UNDERSTANDING VISUAL AND PERFORMING ARTS

FLORIDA GULF COAST UNIVERSITY TEST QUESTIONS

Q. 17. The architect of Fallingwater and the Guggenheim Museum is:

    (a) Louis Sullivan

    (b) Renzo Piano

    (c) Frank Lloyd Wright

    (d) Buckminster Fuller

Q. 23. The ability of a material to withstand crushing is called:

    (a) Compressive Strength

    (b) Tensile Strength

    (c) Post-Tensioned Strength

    (d) Prestressed Strength

Q. 27. Which of the following is the best example of a building design that reflects the natural characteristics of its environment?

    (a) Masonry construction

    (b) Precast

    (c) Litho construction

    (d) Balloon construction

architecture. She told us, "I have to say that has never happened."

Students submit two papers, called "critical analysis essays," which are e-mailed to their preceptors, who read them, append comments, and return them to the students. As all teachers will attest, composing 90 (not to say 300) commentaries is no small task, especially when they must be completed in a matter of days. To ease this problem, Humanities 2510 privately provides its preceptors with a bank of "sample stock comments," which can be downloaded and attached to the papers. Here's one, only slightly abridged:

> Your response would be stronger and more fully developed with the incorporation of more terms from the text. Demonstrating such an awareness in your analysis will assist you in providing a stronger response.

Also, to ensure consistency, preceptors are given sample papers with grades attached so they can conform their own notions of A's and B's to a common template. The Center for Academic Transformation calls aids like these "prepackaged technology solutions." The aim, of course, is to get jobs done faster and to minimize human variations.

For the critical analysis essays, each student must write reviews of an artwork and a performance. Although the campus has a small gallery and offers theatrical productions, the 1,400 members of the class can find their subjects anywhere in the region. We wondered how preceptors who live several states away deal with essays about paintings or plays in the Fort Myers area. How do they assess critiques of performances they haven't seen or art they may not even know of? That wasn't a problem, a preceptor assured us. Her concern is with the intelligence of the analysis, which exists in its own right. But it was her next remark that took us a while to absorb. She said that even if a student hadn't actually gone to a recital and conjured up a program that never took place, if the critique were adroitly done, it would still deserve an A.

Cheating, we were told, is an issue for Humanities 2510. Warnings about plagiarism loom large in the syllabus, with high-tech devices used to detect it. The most common offense is turning in work someone else has written—perhaps a friend who had taken the course a previous semester. However, the odds of getting caught are high. What the students don't know is that every paper that has been submitted since the course started is stored in a databank. So the paper you e-mail is compared with tens of thousands of others to ferret out identical sentences or phrases. We were shown a printout a preceptor had received. At its top, in large type, was emblazoned "*SIMILARITY INDEX: 33%.*" Several "matches" had been flagged to a paper from an earlier year. The preceptor had to decide whether these might have been coincidental. In this case, she wasn't entirely sure, so she simply e-mailed the student a warning. She admitted that something is missing when you suspect cheating and you "can't stare them in the eye." The Florida Gulf Coast databank also links to search engines. So if a student tries to submit some sentences from a newspaper or magazine review, flags will also start waving.

Why so much cheating? The biggest reason, students told us, is that the course calls for huge amounts of memorization. Recall *intaglio, cantilever, ferroconcrete, cantata.* But very few of these undergraduates will be art majors; most are freshmen just out of Florida high schools. They cheat not because they are corrupt or cynical, but from desperation. "There's no way I could keep all that stuff in my head, even with all-nighters of studying," one student said as his friends nodded in agreement. It's not entirely clear here whether the problem was the online delivery of the course—or its basic design. Students need to understand *why* knowing technical terms are necessary to enhance an appreciation of art and architecture and music. Otherwise it's just "stuff." Would it help to see a real instructor twice a week? It would probably depend on the professor—and the design of the course.

In the future, the unseen preceptors—like the section adjuncts they replaced—may find that they too are no longer needed. This may come about because the task of reading papers can be handled by yet another "prepackaged technology solution." In fact, this was tried during the initial years of Humanities 2510. As an experiment, about half of the papers were submitted to a computer program called Intelligent Essay Assessor, which scanned them and graded their arguments. This is not science fantasy. Jim Wohlpart, who was instrumental in getting Humanities 2510 started and is now a Florida Gulf Coast dean, told us he compared computer-given grades with those awarded by human readers on the same set of papers. It turned out that the computers' decisions were actually more consistent, not least because the human graders were more likely to disagree among themselves. Wohlpart's hope is to get the essay assessor back in use.

Florida Gulf Coast showed us studies showing that "student learning" is up, as gauged by the number of correct answers on multiple-choice tests and grades on student papers. With the new course format, there were twice as many A's and B's, and fewer C's or failures. On the economic side, the new version cost only half as much as having adjunct-taught sections. During the semester we visited, tuition fees from the 1,400 students and funds from other sources brought about $540,000 to the course. Pro-rated salaries for the three regular faculty members came to $46,000; an administrative coordinator, who supervises the preceptors from her home in Connecticut, gets $25,000; and stipends for preceptors totaled $35,000. So personnel costs came to a bit over $100,000. Even with hardware and software, and administrative overhead, it struck us that Humanities 2510 makes a tidy profit, which then goes to subsidize more human-intensive courses.

Not all Florida Gulf Coast professors in the arts fields participate in Humanities 2510, and some show no inclination to do so. Insofar as its stated aim is to "build passionate engagement with the arts," they don't see that happening. Anne-Marie Bouche says the students "learn close to nil about art." A colleague called memorizing factoids for multiple-choice answers "a form of mental calesthenics." A student majoring in engineering we spoke to didn't disagree. "The course did not teach me nearly as much as I could have learned in a traditional classroom," he said. "A professor might explain what we could do with all those facts we were memorizing." Still, he saw a value in the course. Later in his career he would be able to nod knowingly when the conversation turned to Debussy or Miró.

Taken together, student reactions were quite positive. On evaluation forms most said they learned a great deal about the subjects and found the assignments mentally challenging. One reason may be that freshmen, who make up most of the enrollment, tend to be less critical during their first college year. And there's the historic fact that today's young people have grown up amid keyboards and screens, and may take it in stride when they find a course in that format. Still, among the relatively small number who took time to write out comments, views tended to the two extremes:

> The course was very stimulating and has encouraged me to learn more about the arts.

> It was a complete waste of time! I did not learn anything.

> The course is designed for cramming and regurgitation of material.

> It made me want to learn. It was also at my own pace. Great job!

> Online courses should cost half as much, seeing how we don't have an "actual" teacher.

> Feedback for essays seem to be complete prefab responses with no real pertinence to the actual essay.

> The class was very enjoyable to me. Overall, the course was informative and the material was interesting.

Given that Humanities 2510 is so entwined with technology, there are already plans to keep it abreast with the times. This, its supporters feel, could do a lot to increase student involvement. With enhanced software, for example, they could call up sequences from an opera or ballet; watch as a sculpture revolves full circle; or take an aerial tour around the Parthenon. Professor Anne-Marie Bouche foresees video games playing out subplots in *Macbeth*; or interactive programs that could call up, say, paintings of Matisse and Warhol the better to analyze them side by side.

At this point, it remains to ask whether Understanding Visual and Performing Arts, as now structured, deserves to be called a college course. On a positive note, all its students have to write analytical papers. Even if they are read and graded from afar, with stock comments, this kind of requirement is not common nowadays for classes of this size. Still, we have to wonder what students absorb about the arts. At no point do they meet face-to-face with a knowledgeable teacher who might help them interpret a fresco, an aria, a soliloquy. On the other hand, not every human teacher is inspiring; indeed, many are incompetent, indifferent, or just burned out. We're open to the notion that in some cases creative software just might do a better job.

More central to the class is its dependence on multiple-choice tests, based on a single textbook. Thus students must review a thousand printed facts to be ready for a question like "Who painted *The Stone Breakers*?" To that extent, they have packed in a lot of precise knowledge, at least of a certain sort. We agree that becoming an educated person requires developing a store of facts. But it hardly needs saying that facts are not sufficient by themselves, whether about art or artists or anything else.

We're trying hard not to say that Humanities 2510 seems close to cramming for a quiz show. But maybe that comparison is also an easy way out. After all, technology only reflects what humans put into it, and the fact-centered design of the course may not be all that different from how introductory courses are already being taught across the nation. And in that sense, perhaps Humanities 2510 reflects the deeper questions that this book has been asking all along about what we want students to learn in college—information? facts? judgment? writing? curiosity?—and whether most college instructors are capable or interested in teaching them.

One thing we do know: given the numbers of students it services, Humanities 2510 is cheap. It seems inevitable that more and more colleges will be installing similar formats, if only because they can't afford more intimate instruction, even at the adjunct level. True, Bowdoin at last report was spending $22,788 on each of its students, and at Pomona it's $32,219. Even so, the great majority of undergraduates will be attending schools like Florida Gulf Coast, where $5,081 is all they have. Since their biggest cost is on-campus instruction, that's where they are deciding to do the cutting. We cannot see how there won't be more variants of Humanities 2510 in higher education's future.

· 12 ·

THE COLLEGE CRUCIBLE:
ADD STUDENTS AND STIR

Quite some time ago, William Bennett, once secretary of education to Ronald Reagan, had an interesting idea:

> Let's take some students of the same social class and IQ, and compare those who go to college with those who don't four years down the road. Let's see how they stack up on things like values and reasoning ability.

A quarter-century has gone by since he came up with this suggestion, so we scoured the research to see if anyone had done such a study. Yet despite endless shelves of books and articles, we found scarcely any addressing the question former secretary Bennett raised. So in this chapter we'll try to fill in at least a few of the gaps.

As we need no reminding, huge amounts of money are invested in going to college. What do students receive in return? The ready answer is of course that you get a degree, which is ostensibly worth something; generally, it will enhance your identity and elevate your status. Yet something more consequential is supposed to happen: you are to become a different, indeed we hope a better, person.

Well, yes, things do happen during those four years. Classes are held, and most students do attend. Tests are given and graded, and often show something has been learned. On some campuses, undergraduates down a lot of beer. At others, they discuss philosophy late into the night. Yet we have little hard information on what college has done for those who have attended. We can assume that students who graduate with majors in accounting come away knowing something about debentures and depreciation. And we know that most graduates expand their earning power: in 2008, holders of bachelor's degrees averaged $47,240, against $28,290 for high school graduates.

The research William Bennett proposed shouldn't be difficult to implement. There are still a lot of high schools where half the graduates go to college and half don't, so it should be possible to find students with comparable backgrounds. For our part, we'd like to look at the people in the sample when they are, say, in their early thirties, so we can see what they've been doing with their lives. But we'd want to know more than their responses to questionnaires or scores on standardized tests. Learning about their occupations would be interesting, as well as how they spend their leisure time, their circles of friends, and general indicators of taste and style. And since our focus is on education, we'd want to see if they differ in how they use their minds as they interpret and perceive the wider world. Even if we find distinctive differences, we would then have to ask how much having been at college was the cause. We don't need research to tell us that years eighteen through twenty-two are a span during which most young people become wiser in the ways of the world, whether or nor they stay with formal schooling.

In his second term, George W. Bush ordered his secretary of education to set up a commission to study higher education and specify how it might be improved. Its report could not be called a vote of confidence. Rather, it echoed a Reagan-era critique of

K–12 schooling, which warned of an impending "rising tide of mediocrity." The Spellings Commission, as it came to be called, concluded that colleges were just as culpable. It charged that today's graduates lacked the skills and information that should be absorbed while earning a bachelor's degree. For example, it reported that from 1992 to 2003, fewer than a dozen years, the number of graduates found to be proficient in reading fell from 37 to 25 percent. Only a fifth of them could do commonplace tasks like computing "the total of an office supply order." Persuaded by these and similar studies, the commission concluded that colleges weren't fulfilling their contract to improve minds and abilities.

In its drafts and a final statement, the commission published a pair of proposals. The first would "require institutions to measure student learning." We would only add our hope that the measurement would be less mechanistic than the mindless testing that characterized Ms. Spellings's "No Child Left Behind" initiative, under which millions of K–12 children and teachers are still staggering. The second would mandate that the "results of such measures" be readily available to college applicants, their parents, and the public as a whole. The report's recurrent theme was *accountability*. Whether a college's fees were high or low, all would have to show what they give in return. More than 1.5 million bachelor's degrees are being awarded annually. If all students were tested in their senior year, their scores could be collated and each institution could get a grade. So everyone would know that Central College received a 68, whereas Seacoast University got an 84. With such reports in hand for all 2,754 four-year schools, the Spellings Commission concluded we would be closer to knowing "whether the national investment in higher education is paying off." We believe this curiosity is legitimate.

We can already hear professors protesting that what they teach is so subtle, so elusive, so ineffable that it can't possibly be assessed by a nationwide test. Indeed, we sympathize with teachers who

challenge their students to think rather than simply absorb information. (We'd only add that we have yet to meet a professor who
doesn't claim to value minds over memorization.)

There has been no shortage of research attempting to tease out
what higher education accomplishes. Indeed, it is a far from
minor industry. The most impressive effort we've seen is a two-
volume compendium called *How College Affects Students*, which
runs on for nearly 1,800 pages, citing over 3,000 articles, books,
and documents, almost all produced by professors. We found
that in itself bemusing—academics wondering if the trade they
themselves ply has palpable results. In the end, three findings
stood out. We'll first list the three together and then examine
them individually.

- The college educated are more knowledgeable and more
  proficient at becoming informed than individuals with only
  a high school education.

- College students learn to think in more abstract, critical,
  complex, and reflective ways.

- College is linked with statistically significant increases in the
  use of principled reasoning to judge moral issues.

On first reading, these statements seem plausible, even convincing. After all, we expect that people who proceed with additional schooling will end up acquiring knowledge. And insofar as
college courses introduce new models and methods, undergraduates must use their minds in unaccustomed ways. And given
academic emphasis on reasoning, students must learn to defend
moral positions they may espouse in essays and examinations.

Yet the more we thought about it, we found ourselves coming
to feel that these findings were, well, too academic. The mental

modes they describe are redolent of syllabuses, assignments, and paper topics. That is, they reflect how professors construe knowledge and interpret reality. So let's take a further look at each of the passages we've just quoted.

> The college educated are more knowledgeable and more proficient at becoming informed than individuals with only a high school education.

We obviously agree that it is better to be more knowledgeable and informed than ignorant or oblivious. But what needs to be plumbed is the *kind* of knowledge that is amassed while pursuing a bachelor's degree. Generally, being better informed is measured by familiarity with facts and interpretations from authoritative sources. Thus it seems safe to assume that college graduates are more likely than others to be able to locate Iran on a map or explain how default credit swaps helped bring on the recent recession.

So we'd like to take being more knowledgeable a step further. Let's turn to a decision that millions of citizens make, and consider the knowledge that goes into it. We have in mind how adults go about deciding for whom they will cast their ballots. In 2008, as it turned out, Barack Obama won the votes of high school and college graduates to exactly the same extent: both groups gave him 53 percent of their support. But should we then presume that the voters in both groups assessed his candidacy in much the same way? After all, they reached the same decision. Or might you want to argue that the ballots of Obama's college supporters were based on more and better information than those of his high school backers? Or that the deliberations leading to their decision were more logical, analytical, and less freighted with bias?

For the moment, we're going to leave these questions hanging, like Florida's electoral chads. Simply posing such questions calls on us to evaluate the quality of people's thinking. Professors do this regularly with their students, evaluating what they say or write. One is given an A and another a C, which are measures of how well they've used their minds, at least in a classroom setting. But assessing the quality of the thought and information behind a vote is rather different. And it brings us back to a question raised early in this book: Does college make people better citizens?

This question leads to the research that claims that, compared with high school graduates,

> College students learn to think in more abstract, critical, complex, and reflective ways.

Indeed, when we asked professors what they hoped to achieve in their teaching, those words—abstract, complex, critical— cropped up in almost every conversation. The predilection academics have for abstractions is well known. So is their bent for stressing the complexity of whatever they study and the methods they use. After all, if what they do were easily understood, it would be difficult to justify research grants and sabbaticals.

But the phrase we encountered most often was "critical thinking." And here, too, our first reaction was, well, yes. No one wants students to stay ingenuous, credulous, or naïve. There are a lot of spurious arguments out there that have a plausible ring. Hence a need to sharpen undergraduates' thinking. Who can object to that?

Here's a question we posed to professors in regard to "critical thinking" during our chats. Imagine, for a paper, that one of your students chose to defend broad use of the death penalty. He or she would argue that eye-for-an-eye is a legitimate reason, that executions of innocents are extremely rare, and that there are statistics to show a deterrent effect. Might such a paper, we asked, feasibly receive an A? Of course it could, we were assured, if its arguments were backed by logic and evidence. Had they, we continued, ever received such a paper and awarded it a high grade? (Or one with similar stances on abstinence education, team prayers, or gun ownership?) Not yet, but there was no reason why it couldn't happen. But we weren't finished. Could you yourself, if we gave you time, draft a pro-death penalty analysis that would satisfy your own A-criteria for critical thinking? Uneasy silences followed, leading us to wonder how much ideology affects how students are assessed.

Whether students' political and social opinions are influenced by what happens at college is itself a subject of public debate. On one side, conservatives claim that most professors are liberal, indeed more conspicuously than in any other profession. Hence, the charge continues, they infuse their ideology into their teaching, whether overtly or by subtle osmosis. Liberals reply that professors respect all points of view and keep their own under wraps. They say that complaints from undergraduates are rare. And of course a wide swath of academic freedom is necessary if higher education is to do its job. On one factual ground, conservatives are correct. A study of professors' party registrations at the Berkeley and Stanford faculties found that Democrats outnumbered Republicans by a ratio of nine to one. Among philosophers, there was a fourteen-to-one tilt; for sociologists, it was almost double that. Only economists, with a three-to-one Democratic edge, came within shouting distance of bipartisan balance. (Nor do we think the results would have been discernibly different at the University of Kansas.)

But how much does four years of exposure to liberal professors affect students' outlooks? Some of the best studies are done by the Pew Research Center, which allows for the nuances inherent in many issues. We chose two topics from the Pew files, the better to compare the responses of high school and college graduates. The first tapped sentiments about abortion. People were given three options: whether the procedure should be banned altogether; whether some limits should be set; or whether abortion should be generally available. The last, the generally available option, was favored by 40 percent of college graduates but only

28 percent of the high school respondents. If generally available and some limits are combined, the results are 67 percent and 43 percent. Clearly, having been at college correlates with a more liberal posture on abortion.

The next Pew question didn't look for opinions, at least not in a direct way. Rather, it asked people for their views on the identities claimed by some of their fellow citizens. How, they were asked, did they explain homosexuality? Here, too, three options were given: do you believe people are born that way; that it results from social or family rearing; or does it express a personal choice? Among the college graduates, 58 percent gave the innate answer, and only 30 percent of the high school group did. On whether homosexuality was a choice, 54 percent of the high school graduates said it was, compared with 32 percent of the college cohort. By any measure, these are significant differences. Although this was posed as a factual question, it really isn't, since no one has hard and fast evidence for any of the answers. What we can say is that college graduates seem to be more relaxed about homosexuality, and their high school counterparts tend to be more unsettled by it.

The knotty question remains whether influences they encountered at college were what led graduates to their more liberal views on abortion and homosexuality. We must confess we don't know. They may have been swayed by professors, or by a campus ambience that places a premium on being open-minded and up to date. Or it's possible that young people who choose college are already in the liberal camp or are readier to embrace that posture.

The third area of research claimed to have found that having been at

> college is linked with statistically significant increases in the use
> of principled reasoning to judge moral issues.

We found ourselves rereading that statement several times. We all acknowledge that life presents moral quandaries, which can test a readiness to make sacrifices for a cause, a principle, or other people. Still, we've seen no evidence that additional education prompts such propensities. So what is it that college graduates are more inclined to be and to do, compared with other citizens? What we understand from the research is that graduates spend more time reasoning about choices they or their communities are called to make.

In his fabled Harvard class on "Justice," Michael Sandel tells of a runaway train hurtling downhill without brakes. A switchman can shunt it toward a group of children or toward three eminent scientists; in either case, death will ensue. Which track should the switchman choose; and, no less crucial since this is Harvard, why?

Vigorous discussions follow, with students urged to apply their minds to making a rational and equitable decision. In theory, we suppose, such intellectualizing might move undergraduates to lead more moral lives. And perhaps anything that slows a rush to judgment is a good thing. But there's another side here: because ratiocination makes issues out to be inexorably complex, it also provides reasons not to take simple steps.

Since humans started voicing their thoughts, "principled reasoning" has been an honorable endeavor. It's why we read Aristotle, Immanuel Kant, and John Rawls. But this doesn't mean that the verbal fluency students attain will necessarily lead them to more selfless lives. On the contrary, it might just be aiding them in justifying less honorable choices. Could a straight line be drawn from the freshman paper on the death penalty to a public relations career, writing press releases arguing that drug company profits are needed to develop lifesaving medicines?

At all events, we agree that holders of bachelor's degrees tend to be more verbal than their less-schooled peers and more adept at crafting paragraphs to justify what they want to do. If those without degrees are more apt to fumble for words, it is often construed as incoherent thinking. We are saddened when this happens. Nor are we sure that it strengthens the case for higher education. In New York City, a workingman jumped onto a subway track to rescue a child who tripped and fell. Asked for a statement afterward, he simply said, "I had to do it." Perhaps deliberation is overrated. We wonder if, had some professors been on the platform, would they have paused to ponder how John Stuart Mill might have parsed the choices?

Whether the United States has a class system, or even can be said to have classes, has long been debated. And probably fruitlessly. People sometimes speak of a "working class" and an "upper class," or "the rich" and "the poor." And then there's the amorphous "middle class," with its upper and lower layers; all of which leads to the question of whether we really know who belongs where. After mulling over these and other puzzles, we decided to cut the class cake one more way. For our purposes, there will be two tiers: adults who have college degrees and the rest who don't. In 2008, the most recent figures at this writing, 33 percent of men and women age twenty-five or older had at least a bachelor's diploma, leaving twice as many—67 percent—without that credential. (Athough it's important to note that about a third of the latter group have spent some time on a campus.)

Completing college is tantamount to having finished a race. If not a marathon, it's still one that's pretty demanding. So let's see why a having degree has become so crucial for employment prospects and social commingling.

- We'll grant that not all the 1.5 million men and women awarded bachelor's degrees each year are serious scholars or avow a love of learning. Even so, they have attended enough classes to win passing grades in a program that satisfied their college's graduation requirements. At the least, it shows they can read and follow rules. Their degrees also show they have fulfilled assignments to the satisfaction of professors, even if tests and term papers were not what they'd rather be doing. They did all this even if many of their classes were listless and much of the teaching was boring. That they continued this pursuit is evidence of resolution, since it extends over several years. And let's not forget that everyone at college is there voluntarily, which is very different from high school.

- College is a middle-class milieu. For those raised in blue-class neighborhoods or modest white-collar settings, it exposes them to new modes of diction and demeanor. And here professors play a role—despite their marginal status in the larger world, they represent and personify a social stratum their students wish to join. Undergraduates who have been raised by college-educated parents—and over half now are—usually aspire to schools designed to propel them even higher. Professors at Stanford and Duke tutor their students in the folkways of America's elites. Indeed, while at college, students recast their conceptions of themselves. We recall a young man at Dartmouth telling us he planned to enter management consulting. Before arriving in Hanover, he hadn't heard of that profession, nor even now was he sure what consultants do. But once there, he learned it was a way to connect with the wealthy and powerful. Whether or not this is Dartmouth's prime purpose, it certainly ranks high.

- College also imparts something subtler. In most college courses, it isn't easy to bluff. The curriculum reveals that there's a lot of abstruse knowledge out there, much of which you can't hope to understand. Thus students come to realize there are times when it's prudent to be cautious; in a word, to keep your mouth shut. And this is a lesson with a long life.

To be found out that you don't know what you're talking about can destroy a career. So the educational divide goes beyond being able to recall the plot of an opera or the cadence of a poet. Listen in first at a blue-collar bar and then at a commuter cocktail lounge. What you're overhearing is a class—and hence a college—difference. It also tells us why cross-class dating, mating, even friendships, seldom work out.

- Of course, in aggregate and average, attending college pays off. Among men aged thirty-five to forty-four, those with bachelor's degrees earn $1,735 for every $1,000 going to those with only a high school diploma. Among women, graduates make $1,864 for each $1,000 their high school peers make. How far these premiums are due to technical skills secured at college isn't easy to know, since social style can also play a role in placements and promotions. Nor is it certain that some colleges are better at imparting styles and skills. A study by Stacy Dale and Alan Krueger surveyed two groups of students. One had attended top-ranked schools; the other group had been accepted at such colleges but for varied reasons had ended up at more average campuses— for example, Brown versus the University of Rhode Island. After graduation, the two groups were found to have similar earnings, which suggests that for good students it doesn't really matter where they go. Indeed, we found much the same outcome when we followed up members of a Princeton class.

It remains to be asked how graduates themselves feel about their college experience. Whether it made them more thoughtful or successful, or for that matter more moral, their own assessments have to count for something. We certainly agree that many regard college as the best years of their lives, and continue to speak fondly of their alma mater. All that granted, we still wanted to know more. So we decided to take as a measure how many graduates contribute to their college's campaigns. As we saw with the Princeton alumni, the appeal is: it doesn't matter what you give, just a symbolic contribution will suffice, since classes are gauged by their participation rate.

For the *U.S. News & World Report* 2010 ratings issue, colleges reported how many graduates had given anything in the previous year. What struck us was how many did not remit even a token $5 check. Forgive us our negativity, but here is a sample of schools, with the percentages who gave nothing at all: Oberlin (59 percent); Colgate (60 percent); Kenyon (62 percent); Lafayette (65 percent); Reed (72 percent); Lewis & Clark (82 percent). Even Princeton, much touted for its loyal alumni, has classes where less than half respond. True, these are only numbers, which never tell the whole story. Even so, they impel us to wonder why a fairly large swath of graduates seem to have less than buoyant memories or otherwise became disaffected.

Of course, the college class isn't miniscule. It's already reached a third of the adult population; among more recent cohorts, it's even higher. Still, it's exclusive enough so that knowing that someone has a degree signals that he or she is one of us, that there's a shared experience. Of course, it's acceptable to ask, "Where did you go?" But so long as you went *somewhere*, having been at Susquehanna College or Sonoma State University will suffice. Once you're moving along in a career, say, by your mid-thirties, there's no reason to be diffident about having attended a less prepossessing school. The notion that there will be a lifelong preferment for Princeton graduates has been supplanted by looking at actual accomplishments. Indeed, the expansion of higher education has had the result the Morrill Act intended: finding talent in new places and releasing that potential.

· 13 ·

SCHOOLS WE LIKE—OUR TOP TEN LIST

Over the years we've been researching this book, people have sometimes asked us: if you had an eighteen-year-old, where would you send your child? It's a great question to which we can only respond that there's no formulaic answer.

The more we pondered, however, the more we realized we did have something to say. First and foremost, we advise parents to think outside of the box. Second, find the exceptions to the system and don't accept conventional thinking. Look for outliers and iconoclasts. Above all, don't get trapped by the accoutrements of prestige, because when it comes to American higher education, price and product are not necessarily related. We think a low cost should be a major determinant in any college decision. After hearing too many horror stories of young people starting off life with six figures of indebtedness, we've come to think that a debt-free beginning is worth far more than a name-brand imprimatur.

Frankly, in a system this vast and varied, there are good people and good schools everywhere; the trick is to find them. What follows are a few places that caught our attention. The list isn't comprehensive, but rather focuses on a few good colleges that strike the right balance. Some of the things the schools we liked had in common: they are student-centered, rather than driven by the whims of the faculty or by administrators' ambitions. We liked schools led by idealists, the only kind of leaders with the courage to buck the conformity that cripples most corners of contemporary higher education. We were drawn to schools that had good core values, for want of a better term, which were genuinely adhered to. Most of all, we preferred schools that actively tried to keep fees low—or free. Confined by financial limitations, their leaders could keep their eyes on what really mattered, which is always the students. At the end of the day, any school must be about putting the "higher" back into education.

OLE MISS: A UNIVERSITY OF RECONCILIATION

We didn't expect to like Ole Miss, the flagship school of the Mississippi public system. If it were possible for an institution of higher learning to be both a symbol and an instrument of segregation, then the University of Mississippi was, for much of its history, exactly that. Before the 1960s civil rights movement transformed America, the planters sent their sons to Oxford to sow wild oats; the daughters attended so that they might find suitable husbands. Under the circumstances, the schooling didn't need to be particularly good. And so, Ole Miss was known for football, beauty queens, and indifferent instruction. And then on October 2, 1962, the Supreme Court ordered the university to admit a black Air Force veteran named James Meredith. In the riots that greeted his admission, two died and dozens were injured. President John F. Kennedy had to send in federal troops.

Today, on campus, there's a statue of James Meredith and Ole Miss is a university where reconciliation and civility are at the very heart of the educational mission. Much of this transformation is the work of Robert Khayat, a remarkable leader, who retired from the chancellorship in 2009. In his fourteen years at Ole Miss, Khayat, himself a former footballer, raised academic standards, tripled the African American enrollment, and banned confederate flags from athletic events—a truly courageous step. But Khayat knew what he had to do if his school was ever to achieve an honorable name. In a sense, Khayat redirected the school's ideology so that it could reach into its past for a different piece of the state's history. Think: Eudora Welty, William Faulkner, Tennessee Williams.

Ole Miss now has a Center for the Study of Southern Culture that focuses on the art, literature, music, and food of the region, black and white. Rowan Oak, Faulkner's home, is an on-campus museum. Rita Bender, the widow of Mickey Schwerner, one of the civil rights workers murdered during the summer of 1964, gives a course in "restorative justice." And did we see correctly at the football game? Was that really a black athlete escorting an extremely white homecoming queen across the field?

When Melissa Cole, a pre-med student in the Barksdale Honors College, first thought about attending Ole Miss, her friends back home in Jackson asked, "Why would you want to go there?" She's African American. Once at Oxford, she got involved with the William Winter Institute for Racial Reconciliation, which she describes as having started much "dialogue of racial reconciliation, racial issues on campus, and how to come together. It's not only black and white, but also international students who are having different experiences." She believes, "Ole Miss has a lot to offer for anybody of any race."

Indeed, of all the flagship schools we visited, we found the University of Mississippi the most appealing. For one thing, the campus very much has the feel of a liberal arts college. Unlike many of the signature universities, you see lots of young people about the campus. This place is actually for them.

Some of this may be due to the fact that the university's medical school is in Jackson and that its research endeavors, generally, are minor. But this is what really sold this university to us: in 2002, a son of James Meredith earned a doctorate from the University of Mississippi's School of Business Administration. "I think there's no better proof that white supremacy was wrong than not only to have my son graduate, but to graduate as the most outstanding graduate of the school," James Meredith Sr. said. "That, I think, vindicates my whole life."

RARITAN VALLEY: A COMMUNITY COLLEGE THAT COULD

As we drove up to it, we could see Raritan Valley Community College's signature feature, a sprawling parking lot, large enough for a regional shopping center. That's because it's situated in exurban New Jersey, far from any major city and certainly not served by public transportation. So its 9,971 students get there in almost as many cars, mostly coming for one or two classes and then departing to a job. Half the students are part-time, usually in fields like Respiratory Care, Electrical Utility Technology, or Food and Beverage Management. In this, Raritan is much like the nation's other 2,169 two-year colleges.

But in one way, the school is different from many of the others in its tier. Raritan offers a full-fledged version of college freshman and sophomore years. Each year, several hundred of its students transfer to become juniors not only in New Jersey institutions but increasingly across the country. Indeed, this is why we want to tell you about Raritan. In our view, it provides a better introduction to college work than many four-year schools.

For starters, it has no mega-lectures. Its classes don't exceed forty students, and many are seminar size. Team teaching is encouraged, with both professors present throughout the semester. Kevin Reilly told us he recently joined in an integrated course in World History and World Literature, which he and a colleague taught to twenty-two students, mainly freshmen. Since it's entirely a teaching faculty, promotions don't hinge on publications. Everyone on the full-time staff teaches five courses per semester—that's double Kenyon's load. Almost all the faculty in the liberal arts fields have doctorates, albeit from second-tier schools like Northeastern, Binghamton, and Delaware. But from everything we saw and heard, they are committed to their students. Their particular mission is to get them ready to excel when they move on to a bachelor-degree college.

Tuition at Raritan is $3,750 per year. That's about all you'll need, apart from maintaining a car. But you have to live at home, or find an apartment to share, and contrive a social life with classmates who disperse in many directions. Still, it is a college, with a library, dining facilities, and a swimming pool. Plus there are six athletic teams with serious schedules; women's basketball plays twenty-seven games. Student associations include an Astronomy Club, Amnesty International, Campus Crusade for Christ, and a Social Justice Club. How much more does a student need? "Even if we don't have much of a campus," Kevin Reilly says, "you can find kindred spirits and create a stimulating life for yourself."

Like all two-year colleges, Raritan's classes are taught mainly by adjuncts. More precisely, its 97 full-time professors are backstopped by 304 part-timers who show up for a course or two. Many have been with Raritan for quite a while, are good in their fields, and can work closely with students because classes are small. But we'll be frank: they don't have offices or even a desk of their own. Still, students who figure out how the college works plan their programs around full-time professors.

The signal fact about Raritan and colleges like it is that you can get a start with the liberal arts at a tenth of the cost of many private tuitions, and a third of what flagship colleges are charging. More than that, you can learn with professors who know your name and have an interest in your future. Of course, after those two congenial years, the price of higher education rises, with a likelihood of loans to foot higher tuitions and living expenses. Still, for young people with limited budgets, we recommend community colleges as a place to begin. They are not just centers for vocational training; they also set and achieve high standards in the arts and sciences.

UNIVERSITY OF NOTRE DAME: FOR BEING TRUE TO ITSELF

We were at a dinner in New York City where journalists were invited to meet interesting university and college presidents. At one point, a reporter asked why so many campuses looked more like Ritz-Carltons than centers of learning. "We don't do that," remarked a man sitting at the far end of the table. The speaker was the Reverend John I. Jenkins, C.S.C., president of the University of Notre Dame since 2005. "Our facilities are pretty basic." In fact, the Notre Dame campus looks Spartan when compared to that of a Williams or Dartmouth. But that's part of the school's appeal. Perhaps because of its religious base, the school has successfully avoided the faddish academic trends and the compulsive consumerism that have overwhelmed many other colleges.

Notre Dame is often called "the Catholic Harvard." And yes, it's hard to get into. But that's where the comparison ends. Teaching appears to have genuine import at Notre Dame. The school's Mission Statement tells the story:

> The University seeks to cultivate in its students not only an appreciation for the great achievements of human beings, but also a disciplined sensibility to the poverty, injustice, and oppression that burden the lives of so many. The aim is to create a sense of human solidarity and concern for the common good that will bear fruit as learning becomes service to justice.

We like what that statement implies. We also like that Notre Dame has a twelve-to-one student-faculty ratio and that only 7 percent of the classes are taught by graduate assistants. We like it that the university's president, Oxford-educated philosopher John Jenkins, has himself taught undergraduates—and that he personally counsels them if they are suffering a spiritual crisis.

Interestingly, for a university famous for football, sports don't seem to overwhelm. On Notre Dame's website, it is academics and student life that are trumpeted. It's as if the administrators here are saying, "Listen, we have our priorities."

And one of them is academic freedom. In 2004, the school invited the European Islamic theologian Tariq Ramadan to teach. But then, at the last moment, the Bush administration's Department of Homeland Security withdrew Ramadan's visa on antiterrorism grounds that it refused to share with the American public. Notre Dame's answer was unequivocal. Said Matthew V. Storin, associate vice president: "It's unfortunate that we were not able to have him share his views with our students because the idea was to have dialogue in the interest of peace. You want to have as many divergent voices as you can."

More controversy yet was heard in June 2009, when the university invited the president of the United States to give the commencement speech. Because Barack Obama had been elected on a pro-choice platform, this irked some anti-abortion conservatives. For weeks, Reverend Jenkins was denounced and pressured to rescind the invite. His answer to the angry voices: "You cannot change the world if you shun the people you want to persuade, and if you cannot persuade them, show respect for them and listen to them." That steadfastness makes John Jenkins worth every penny of the $475,000 he earns each year, which, interestingly, he donates completely back to the university.

THE COOPER UNION—GREATNESS FOR FREE

A decade ago, when the Cooper Union for the Advancement of Science and Art, an all-scholarship school for the nation's most promising engineering, fine arts, and architecture students, was in financial trouble, some trustees suggested that tuition be instituted. The school was founded by philanthropist Peter Cooper in 1859 and he mandated that it be "as free as the air and the water." "We were in desperate financial straights in 2000–2001," Cooper's president, Dr. George Campbell Jr., told us at a luncheon in 2009, "but we couldn't seriously think about doing that."

Instead, the school sold off some land it owned. "Real estate isn't as important as our tradition. Maintaining free tuition was what mattered," Campbell says. While many Ivies describe themselves as meritocracies, Cooper Union actually is one. Art and architecture applicants are considered not by their SAT scores, but through a "home test" of six of ten open-ended questions. "We're looking to see how a student conceptualizes," reports the admissions dean, Mitchell Lipton, "as opposed to their technical abilities. The nice part about this test is that we can find a diamond in the rough." Eleanor Baum, Cooper's engineering dean, reaches out to public and parochial schools, especially those where smart immigrants are studying. By working with guidance counselors, she showed potential applicants that they could obtain a profession in four instead of seven or eight years—as might be the case if they did law or medicine. Many high-scoring young females became interested. Special open-house evenings where the girls and their families met female engineers who spoke of work and family issues closed the deal. Without lowering standards the dean has managed to build an engineering class that is at least 50 percent female.

At Cooper, not a penny is wasted on frills. As we noted in an earlier chapter, the total athletics budget is $20,000 a year. Not surprisingly this meritocracy has produced some noteworthy graduates: Daniel Libeskind, the architect of Berlin's Jewish Museum; Elizabeth Diller and Ricardo Scofido, the creators of New York's High Line; Kevin Burke, the CEO of Con Edison; artist Alex Katz; cartoonist Edward Sorel; and Nobelist Russell Hulse, who discovered the binary pulsar.

When undergraduates from the Cooper Union sit around a table and talk about their futures, their tone is very different from students we've met elsewhere. Yes, they are getting an unusually good education and they know it, but their lack of debt changes everything. Not one utters that painful phrase we've heard from Maine to Montana: "I'd like to . . . but I've got these loans."

BEREA COLLEGE—A GREAT TRADITION

If we sensed that history hung like a shroud of Spanish moss over Ole Miss, there's a completely different feeling to Kentucky's Berea College. At Berea, the past is the key to a democratic mission that is still heartfelt today. This liberal arts college, rated by a *U.S. News & World Report* survey as one of "the best comprehensive" colleges in the South, was founded in the nineteenth century by radical Christian abolitionists who wanted to create a center in Appalachia where talented young people of all races could learn together. Like Cooper Union, Berea has never charged tuition. Instead, students are asked to contribute ten hours a week of labor. Most of its 1,500 scholars come from the top 20 percent of their high schools and from families where the annual income is under $50,000 a year. In that way, it's the anti-Harvard. "We think students are worth more than the tuition they can afford," declares a mission statement on the school's website.

Indeed, Berea's totally free application is a revelation. It doesn't ask if you have gone off to work with the poor of Paraguay, it asks if you are poor! From a checklist to prospective Berea applicants: "Please check all aid that your household receives below—Supplemental Security Income, SSI, Food Stamps, Free or Reduced School Lunch Program, Temporary Assistance for Needy Families."

For those fortunate enough to win admission, a first-rate education is proffered. The student faculty ratio is ten-to-one with no graduate teaching assistants substituting for real professors.

Among its alumni are John Fenn, winner of the 2002 Nobel Prize in Chemistry; Juanita Kreps, the former U.S. Secretary of Commerce; and Tony Award winner Tharon Musser. An earlier graduate was James Bond, a former slave and the great-grandfather of Julian Bond, a former chair of the National Association for the Advancement of Colored People (NAACP). "My father often spoke of Berea," Julian Bond told us—his father was Horace Mann Bond, the president of Lincoln University. "He spoke of how when James Bond was fifteen and still nearly illiterate, he hitched his tuition—a steer—to a rope and walked him several miles to Berea. And they let him in! It's a great story."

ARIZONA STATE UNIVERSITY: BIG AND EXCITING

There's a marvelous energy to Arizona State University in Tempe, a feeling of busyness that is at once exciting and overwhelming. At a distance, ASU—with its 68,000 students and 250 undergraduate programs—seems like just another oversized state school: a giant credential factory with a football team. But take a closer look and one quickly sees that Arizona State may well be the most experimental institution in the country, a university where the old rules are up for grabs and where anyone with an interesting idea can get a hearing. Arizona State can seem near the ultimate megaversity, yet despite all our objections to the concept we find the vibrancy and the choices available to students there tremendously exciting. At Arizona State, there's always a three-ring circus going on. The university offers so many schools and programs that a freshman will have a hard time picking from the smorgasbord of possibilities.

Here are a few of the surprises we discovered at ASU:

- The Barrett Honors College offers three thousand undergraduates the intimacy of a liberal arts college, at state school prices. Barrett has its own dining facilities, dorms, and special seminars.

- ASU has not one but two engineering schools. In addition to the traditional mathematics-based school in Tempe, there's a second—the Polytechnic, which is for tinkerers and inventors as opposed to math whizzes. It's located on a decommissioned air force base in the desert town of Chandler. On the day we visited, students were trying to turn bacterial slime into automotive fuel.

- The university is rebuilding the city of Phoenix. Five schools were moved from the main campus in Tempe into downtown Phoenix, where they've brought new life, people, and businesses to what had been a dying city center. The Walter Cronkite School of Journalism is now within walking distance of the *Arizona Republic* and the local NBC television station. Synergy abounds.

And there's more. At ASU, many of the academic departments have been dissolved and re-formed within new interdisciplinary institutes, breaking the stranglehold of the disciplines that is so deadly at most schools.

All of these revolutions are the brainchild of Michael Crow, perhaps the most creative university president on the contemporary scene. He came to Arizona in 2002 from Columbia University, where he'd been executive vice provost. Arizona State has proved a fantastic workshop for Michael Crow's ideas.

Though ASU was the second-tier school within a frankly third-rate public system, the political elite of Arizona wanted to improve it. Whereas many top educators have contentious relations with their state legislatures, Crow won massive support from the state, federal government, and the city of Phoenix. His argument? Arizona will be forever tossed by instability if the economy remains tied to tourism and construction. Build up the university, invest in an educated workforce, and the Phoenix area can become the new Singapore.

A great deal of Crow's argument involved turning ASU into a research powerhouse, an idea we support in this case because it would draw clean, brainy enterprises to a region that has virtually none. Crow's grand plans were just beginning to jell when the Sun Belt's economy tanked with the housing meltdown. To keep the doors open, Crow instituted draconian economics and raised tuition, but nonetheless, the growth of this university remains one of the few bright spots in Arizona's otherwise bleak financial picture.

When we met with a group of Barrett Honors College students they struck us as bright as any we met at Ivy League schools. Indeed, many had been accepted to such schools, but they'd opted for Arizona State instead. Charlene Shovic said she enjoyed ASU because "I've found that coming here, my eyes have been opened to more varieties of people, places and experiences than if I'd gone to a small, really expensive school. A lot of my friends who went to places like Amherst seem really sheltered to me now."

Of course, not all of ASU is paradise. We heard undergraduates in the regular four-year college complain about oversized classes and sometimes indifferent professors who'd grown arrogant with time and tenure.

But on the whole, the desert air around Tempe is invigorating. We love the sense of adventure that permeates the culture. Good, bad, smart, stupid, it's possible to get new things started at Arizona State. Even some old-time professors, none of them necessarily Michael Crow fans, told us that they found it exciting to be working at an institution with so much buzz. Their willingness to accept a reformer and go with a new institutional culture made us think that many academics might actually prefer more challenging work environments than the ones they've grown used to.

UNIVERSITY OF MARYLAND, BALTIMORE COUNTY—MELDING TEACHING AND RESEARCH

In an earlier chapter we introduced the University of Maryland, Baltimore County, where the Meyerhoff Scholarship program has greatly increased the number of African Americans in the biological sciences and engineering. But UMBC is an interesting school for another reason. Though it is a PhD-granting research university centered on science and engineering, undergraduate instruction is anything but an afterthought. Good teaching, at all levels, is sincerely emphasized. Of all the research universities we visited, UMBC was the place that we thought had most capably connected its research functions with undergraduate schooling.

And the *U.S. News & World Report* survey agrees. It has listed UMBC as fourth among the best universities for under-graduate education, ahead of Brown, Duke, Berkeley, and the University of Chicago. When we visited the campus, we were struck by how many of the students were enthusiastic about their education. Two honors college undergraduates, Philip Graff and Christianna Stavroudis, said they'd developed strong personal relationships with their professors. Brian Hodges reported that he'd originally been accepted by several of the Ivies. As a minor-ity athlete with a fine high school record, he was exactly who they wanted, though not enough to offer him a full scholarship. Rather than burden his parents with debt, Hodges opted for UMBC because it was local, offered lots of financial aid, and had Freeman Hrabowski at the helm. "On my first visit to the school I had the opportunity to meet the president, which was a huge thing to me," Hodges said.

Dr. Hrabowski's leadership style is certainly a big factor in UMBC's undergraduate success. He sets a tone from the top that says teaching undergraduates is important, and the faculty knows he means it.

MASSACHUSETTS INSTITUTE OF TECHNOLOGY:
DIGNITY AND DOLLARS TO PART-TIMERS

It's good to adjunct at MIT, the prestige science, mathematics, and engineering mecca that abuts Harvard in Cambridge. Marcia Bartusiak, a master's degree physicist and the author of such books as *Thursday's Universe* and *Einstein's Unfinished Symphony*, works at the school's Graduate Program of Science Writing as a half-time adjunct professor. What that means is that she teaches two and a half courses a year and coordinates internships. For that, she earns half the pay of a regular professor—plus benefits for five contract years. Though she demurred from divulging figures, our estimate is that half an MIT's associate professor's package is in the neighborhood of $70,000.

MIT also employs a less rich category of part-timer—instructors who get $8,000 and up per course. If they teach two or more classes, they are eligible for health insurance, making MIT the contingents' Valhalla. So far as we've heard, decency, fair pay, and health insurance have yet to bankrupt the school. It wouldn't at other institutions, either.

WESTERN OREGON UNIVERSITY: AN OUTLIER
THAT SUCCEEDS

On a Sunday drive through the Northwest, we had difficulty finding the hamlet of Monmouth, population 7,741, the home of Western Oregon University. After many wrong turns on ill-marked roads, we ended up in a one-traffic light/one-motel town, where the local diner stopped serving at nine. Even the police station was shuttered. But when the sun came up the next day, we discovered an educational jewel: a school without any frills or pretense, that did its job with utter seriousness and dedication.

This former teachers college is actually typical of how most Americans get their higher education; not from name-brand schools but from smaller regional branches of their state's public system. At Western Oregon, the name of the game is making a good education available to those who never could access it before. Most of the school's nearly six thousand students are either rural or working class; a majority are the first in their families to ever attend college. Because Western Oregon's administrators view themselves as facilitators of social mobility, costs are kept at a minimum. Tuition is about a thousand dollars a year less than it would be at the better known University of Oregon or Oregon State University. The school even offers a "tuition promise" to entering freshmen: their fees will remain unchanged throughout their four years in Monmouth.

And for every student we met, money truly mattered. Many were working at jobs while pursuing their degrees. Several told of studying between midnight and four in the morning. So the university administrators try to keep prices low. Although the campus is attractive and modern, there are few of the bells and whistles that have become routine at other schools. Faculty salaries are low, in the $45,000 to $75,000 range. That's for three courses in a semester. There are no star professors, not much research, and the administration is bare bones.

All these limits inadvertently make Western Oregon a delightful place. The austerity gives people a chance to look each other in the eye and talk. At Western Oregon, low status and low budgets mean that all energy is focused on one thing: educating the undergraduates.

We particularly liked the faculty we met. They'd trained at good schools—UCLA, Cornell, Carnegie Mellon, Baylor, the University of Wisconsin—and had landed in Monmouth by surprise, fate, or the vagaries of the PhD glut. By truly being where they were, these professors were innovative educators—plus they were having fun. Sociologist Peter Callero came to Western Oregon in 1986. Though he had plenty of publications on his vita, he was sick of working at research universities where the students were a footnote. Once in Monmouth, Callero discovered that he could get creative with his teaching. In addition to the standard sociology and criminology courses, Callero and his colleague Dr. Dean Braa designed a two-semester sequence, Community Organizing and Community Action. In the first term, the students read Saul Alinsky and Stanley Aronowitz. In the second, the kids went out into Monmouth and organized a tenants' union.

Most of Western Oregon's offerings, however, are more conventional. The menu is basic but hearty: earth science, literature, anthropology, biology, philosophy—with social work, law enforcement, and nursing credits possible. There's one honors college for the best of the four-year students and there's a second for those who come in after two years at the local community colleges.

And such an ethos makes the professors different. Though they are poorly paid, they aren't complainers. It was Peter Callero who said something to us that we rarely heard from a professor in all our travels: "I love these students. Teaching is a high for me."

Later that day, we saw why. As it happened, we had come to Monmouth on Martin Luther King Jr.'s birthday. The students had organized a dinner in his memory. A young woman, Mexican American, the winner of an essay contest, stepped forward to read her piece about what Dr. King meant to her. As a single mother, she had already lived many hardships. Dr. King had preached the theology of hope, of having a chance for a better future, "the content of their character . . ." and she hoped to prove him right. In that moment, we saw something special: Western Oregon State and the opportunity it offered to many of society's neglected was the actual fulfillment of all that Martin Luther King Jr. had dreamed.

EVERGREEN STATE COLLEGE—THE RULE BREAKER

If Arizona State University is a fascinating top-down experiment, then Evergreen State College, in Olympia, Washington, gets our attention for its inventive style, though this school does it in a far more communal way. This liberal arts school is very much a product of the 1960s, when the state of Washington decided to create a new type of public college, one rooted in the ideas of the progressive education movement. John Dewey would love Evergreen. The deans are elected. There are no grades, no set curriculum. At the end of each quarter, professors present students with long written evaluations of their work; the students, in turn, do the same for their teachers. Courses are cross-disciplinary and team-taught and they are invented or redesigned annually.

Though one might think that Evergreen's democratic governance would create a gridlock, it doesn't. The place draws students, faculty, and administrators who buy into its values, and so the school is infused with a sense of commonality of purpose. At Evergreen we saw something we'd never seen anywhere else: a philosophy professor giving a lecture to his class on a usual topic, and other teachers stopping by to listen.

A biology professor told us about how she was hired: "I answered an ad in the *Chronicle,* without knowing much about the school. When I got here for the interview, instead of having me present my research, they asked me to lecture on 'Aging,' not at all my subject. They wanted to see my intellectual depth. I thought, 'Wow, this is different.'"

The students are different, too. When we put a call out for students to tell us about their experiences, about twenty turned up, bursting with stories to tell about their schooling. They were slightly older than usual, in their early and mid-twenties, transfers from other schools, smart, mature, more self-confident than youngsters we'd met elsewhere. Their teachers, one told us, "were very invested" in their success. One student said that he's "never had a bad teacher." Another said that there were some duds among the faculty, but "everyone here is passionate about something."

We liked Emily Scoemi, a transfer student who'd started out

at Bennington, dropped out, worked for five years, and then finished up at Evergreen: "People say that you don't get job training
here. Speaking with my peers in academic seminars is job training. In the future, I'll be evaluated one-on-one with bosses and
employees and lovers and friends. That's the most valuable thing
I'll get out of Evergreen—being able to communicate."

Of course, despite its reputation as a countercultural bastion,
Evergreen grads do find jobs. One of the more famous alums is
Matt Groening, the genius behind *The Simpsons*. According to
Evergreen's own statistics, 82 percent of the school's graduates
found full-time employment within a year. Of those who applied
to graduate schools, 93 percent were admitted. Even without formal grades, graduates get into medical schools, though it took
Dean Paul Przybylowicz a while to convince admissions officers
that Evergreen's intensive narrative evaluations would tell them
more than a simple lettered grade. Evergreen's science program is
well regarded.

However, Evergreen is not the school for everyone. The shy,
the lost, the unfocused will sink in an atmosphere where you are
expected to set your own intellectual goals. Some of the teaching
is bad, though there are mechanisms to fix it, which makes Evergreen different from 95 percent of America's colleges. There's
also a boring amount of political correctness reflected in some
course titles, though in reality the classes are quite substantive.
For those who want to spend four years in an atmosphere of pure
learning, this is the school. Plus it's one of the unheralded public
liberal arts colleges in the country, which means that it's possible
to get a small-school education at a fraction of the price.

The answer to the question "Where would you send your
child to college?" is any of these schools would work fine for us.

CODA

Soon after we embarked on writing *Higher Education?* we found ourselves concluding that our colleges and universities had lost track of their basic mission. A huge—and vital—sector of our society had become a colossus, taking on many roles, and doing none of them well. Our nation's young people deserve better than the overpriced and undernourished diet they are being fed. Nor is higher educational reform about beating the Chinese on mathematics scores. It's about how we view our obligations to our next generation. As with health care, we are confronting a sector of society so vast, so diverse, that no one change is likely to overhaul it. Still, here are a few proposals we think might start to set things right.

THE PURPOSE OF HIGHER EDUCATION IS EDUCATION

Since the purpose of higher education is—yes—education, all other activities should be made to justify why they exist on campuses at all. Examples of extraneous activities that impede teaching and learning include new administrative officers (like a "director of collaborative engagement"); varsity athletics (the University of Vermont sends its softball team 2,533 miles to play against Stanford); and undergraduate amenities (five-story climbing walls). Top-heavy faculties should also be scrutinized (75 percent at Stanford have lifetime appointments, as do 73 percent at San Jose State) since senior professors are less involved with teaching.

STOP RELYING ON LOANS

Costs attributed to the aforementioned activities, staff, and faculty have raised tuition well ahead of the consumer price index. Unlike in the past, students are borrowing to pay most of their bills, a system we would like to see dismantled. Parents are part of the problem, especially if they've been listening to Suze Orman, who tells them "no parent should have to be responsible for financing his or her child's education." At Ohio Wesleyan, 77 percent of students graduate in debt, as do 85 percent at Hollins University. Even wealthy Williams has told scholarship students they will have to take out loans. After interest and penalties, repayments can reach three times the face amount, making this the first generation of young people to embark on adulthood in debt.

ENGAGE ALL STUDENTS

We believe all Americans are capable of college work, so universal enrollment should be our ultimate goal. But for this to happen, professors will have to make an effort to reach their students; not, as William Bennett once said, "teach their dissertation or next article." This can be done. The University of Tennessee offers small seminars for its 4,250 entering freshmen, with professors who have volunteered to teach them. Some topics have included "How to Think Like Leonardo da Vinci," "Football Physics," and "Ethical Issues in Animal Research."

"We ask professors to display their own passion for learning," Todd Daicon, the program's director, told us. Note how the topics skirt traditional disciplines. Colleges should demand good teaching: conscientious, caring, and attentive to every corner of their classrooms.

MAKE STUDENTS USE THEIR MINDS

What should happen to students during their years at college? Our answer is simple: we'd like them to become more thoughtful and interesting human beings. Undergraduates should be exposed to exciting intellects, who will challenge them to use their minds as they never have before. However, well over half—some 64 percent—of undergraduates are currently enrolled in vocational majors. We wish this weren't so. We would like to persuade them that supposedly impractical studies are a wiser use of college years and ultimately a better investment.

Instead of philosophy, literature, and history, or the physical sciences, most undergraduates are now choosing fields like equine management, welding technology, and fashion merchandising, all majors at reputable colleges. The undergraduate years are an interlude that will never come again, a time to liberate the imagination and stretch one's intellect without worrying about a possible payoff. We'd like this for everyone, not just the offspring of professional parents.

TENURE SERVES NO USEFUL PURPOSE

Lifelong tenure should be abolished and replaced by multiyear contracts. Despite fears concerning academic freedom, we have concluded that higher education will lose nothing by ending this perquisite and will reap major gains.

Tenure takes a huge toll at every academic level, impacting all aspects of college life. To start, professors who possess it have no reason to improve their teaching, take on introductory courses, or, in fact, accept any tasks not to their liking. A brutal price is paid by junior faculty. No other profession has this all-or-nothing prize, essentially decreeing professional life or death. Caution takes charge. Cristina Nehring, a UCLA doctoral candidate, notes that the struggle for tenure "rewards conformity over achievement, collegiality over originality, quantity over quality." Rather than enhancing academic freedom, the tenure quest actually subverts it. If there were only one reform we could achieve, this would be it.

FEWER SABBATICALS, LESS RESEARCH

Paid sabbaticals should be ended. For their part, colleges should cease requiring research from their faculties. If professors are burning to write books, they have long summers and three-day weekends.

One mantra is that academics need every seventh year to recharge their mental batteries. We've found no evidence that this happens during a sojourn in Tuscany. We next hear that relief from teaching is needed to better conduct their *research*. We have argued that few of these accretions are needed; on the contrary, most are contrived to embellish careers. Since upward of 500,000 assistant, associate, and full professors are now eligible for sabbaticals, do we really need that many new books or articles?

END EXPLOITATION OF ADJUNCTS

It is immoral and unseemly to have a person teaching exactly the same class as an ensconced faculty member, but for one-sixth the pay. Adjuncts should receive the same per-course compensation as an assistant professor, including health insurance and other benefits. Teaching assistants' unions should be recognized as a step for winning them a living wage.

Most of these adjuncts are committed teachers who were over-produced by PhD factories, more politely called graduate schools. But their job isn't easy; they have no offices, often not even a desk; and many commute to several campuses. Finding money to eradicate this outcast group should have highest priority—higher, certainly, than a new campus in Abu Dhabi or a mega-athletic complex in Stillwater.

DEMAND THAT THE GOLDEN DOZEN DELIVER

The colleges we call the Golden Dozen have become an academic Olympus. We believe their reputations need to be reconsidered as their special status is often overrated and in many respects undeserved.

While as good an education can be had at Earlham and Vanderbilt as at Amherst or Yale, some facts cannot be ignored. Top law schools are impressed by Dozen degrees and are more apt to accept their graduates. And elite professional credentials lead to better entry jobs. Even so, we found that most Dozen graduates do not create distinctive lives and careers—at least not to the extent one would expect from colleges that claim to find and nurture unusual talent. Graduates of Haverford and Davidson are nearly twice as likely to end up in *Who's Who in America* as products of Duke or Brown or Penn.

Parents need to help by ceasing to demand brand-name schools—which may reflect their own status-seeking rather than a concern for their children—and start looking beyond the conventional labels.

PRESIDENTS AS PUBLIC SERVANTS

Presidents should say "thanks, but no thanks" if their trustees offer them salaries of $1 million, or anything near it. Or when recruiters say they'll try to get that much.

We were often told that colleges must pay to get the best administrative skills. This generally means raising money, overseeing a bureaucracy, and ensuring athletic programs don't go embarrassingly awry. We're not opposed to talent, but higher education needs something more. A salary—certainly one running to seven figures—is a symbol. We believe people who choose higher education should view it as a *public service*. The head of the Food and Drug Administration puts in a full day for $199,700, as do four-star generals for $151,900. We're not proposing that college leaders take vows of poverty, but do they really need quasi-corporate stipends to take the job?

SPIN OFF MEDICAL SCHOOLS AND RESEARCH CENTERS

Universities should consider cutting ties with medical schools, as well as research centers and institutes now situated on their campuses. Postgraduate training has a place, so long as it doesn't divert faculties from working with undergraduates or preoccupy university presidents, who should be musing about education, not angling for another center on antiterrorist technologies. For people who want to do research, plenty of other sites exist, such as the Brookings Institution, the Rand Corporation, and the Howard Hughes Medical Institute, all of which do excellent work without university ties. Princeton University has succeeded quite nicely, including in the sciences, without a medical school—which soon becomes the most costly complex on a campus, commandeering resources and attention. In fact, the "school" is a minute part of it. Johns Hopkins has only 473 medical students, but atop them sits an empire with 32,700 employees.

A HEARING FOR TECHNO-TEACHING

Nothing outshines a superb teacher, whether in small seminars or large lecture halls. But we've been hearing that a living presence can be usefully supplemented; in some cases, even replaced. Our first reaction was suspicion—but then we found we wanted to know more.

We realize that the chief impetus behind techno-teaching—as we're tempted to call it—is to cut costs. Human instructors, even adjuncts, can be expensive. However, a gripping performance on a screen may be preferable to a live teacher of doubtful competence. Unlike a textbook, software can pose interactive questions, review answers, and tell students to try again, offering hints on where they may have gone wrong. Other computer programs can meld clips from movies, plays, or ballet; set paintings side by side; or present aerial tours showing climate changes. We agree that techno-teaching can't rival a seminar pondering *Moby Dick* or *King Lear.* But until we improve classroom instruction, these new methods shouldn't be dismissed out of hand.

SPREAD DONATIONS AROUND

In the higher tiers of education, the watchword is "to them that hath, shall be given." All too many benefactors prefer to donate to colleges that are already well provided for. Perhaps we're naïve, but we'd like to see this changed.

Even in economic downturns, gifts to the wealthiest schools keep coming in, well beyond what they can reasonably use. So here's a suggestion for their alumni and other donors: pick another college—there's a long deserving list—and send your check where it will truly do some good. Several years ago, Conan O'Brien returned to Harvard to address the graduating class. He noted his alma mater had just raised $2.6 billion, but he still received soliciting calls. "What do you need it for?" he asked the agent. From the other end: "We don't need it. We just want it."

SOURCES

Much of the background material in *Higher Education?* was obtained from the following sources: U.S. Department of Education, U.S. Census, Bureau of Labor Statistics, College Board, Educational Testing Service, Center for Academic Transformation, National Survey of Student Engagement, Integrated Postsecondary Education Data System, National Collegiate Athletic Association, American Association of University Professors, *Digest of Education Statistics*, *U. S. News & World Report*, *Barron's Profile of American Colleges*, *Princeton Review's 371 Best Colleges*, the *New York Times*, *Chronicle of Higher Education*, *Inside Higher Education*, *Adjunct Nation*, Seeley Mudd Library of Princeton University, Christopher Langdell Library of Harvard Law School, and the websites of the colleges we studied—that's how we found that Stanford offers 229 history courses and Williams will provide birthday cakes for its students.

NOTES

5   *job-training program*: Diane Ravitch as quoted in Derek Bok, *Our Underachieving Colleges* (Princeton University Press, 2008), 3.

5   *informed citizen*: Bok, *Our Underachieving Colleges*, 8.

6   *to become leaders*: Shirley Tilghman's commencement speech, "In Pursuit of Purpose and Learning," reprinted in the *Princeton Alumni Weekly*, July 15, 2009.

26   *to purchase a*: "Mortgage Assistance Program document," Stanford University Office of the Provost Faculty Staff Housing, 1. A PDF version is available at http://fsh.stanford.edu/images/ MAP.pdf.

29   *84 athletic coaches*: *The Williams Directory, 2006–2007*, 5–6.

32   *Lourdes College*: "Special Supplement on Campus Architecture," *Chronicle of Higher Education*, March 25, 2005.

41   *a lot of energy*: Shirley Jackson as quoted in Audrey Williams June, "Shirley Ann Jackson Sticks to the Plan," *Chronicle of Higher Education*, June 15, 2007.

41   *hired guns*: Patrick Callan as quoted in Paul Fain and Audrey Williams June, "The Bottom Line for College Presidents," *Chronicle of Higher Education,* November 24, 2006.

42   *$2,513 for a limousine*: Harry Jaffe, "Ben Ladner's Years of Living Lavishly," *Washingtonian,* April 1, 2006.

45   *quiz program*: "Too Many Eager Beavers?" *Time,* November 10, 1947.

53   *the working poor*: Jeffrey J. Selingo, "University Official Knocks Treatment of Adjuncts," *Chronicle of Higher Education,* October 14, 2008.

55   *system for preparing*: Rachel Dempsey, "Preparation of TAs Varies Greatly," *Yale Daily News,* December 6, 2006.

58   *levels of commitment*: Paul D. Umbach, "How Effective Are They?" *The Review of Higher Education* 30, no. 2 (Winter 2007).

58   *dropout rates*: M. Kevin Eagan Jr. and Audrey J. Jaeger, "Effects of Exposure to Part-time Faculty on Community College Transfer," *Research in Higher Education* 50, no. 2 (March 2009).

65   *only a third*: "College Profile," *Groton School Quarterly,* September 2005.

80   *commanding attention*: Michael Sandel as quoted in Ken Bain, *What the Best College Teachers Do* (Harvard University Press, 2004), 109.

82   *I have failed*: John Lachs as quoted in Bain, *What the Best College Teachers Do,* 145.

83   *be a good teacher*: Michael J. Hogan in "The Provost's Perspective," *Parent Times,* University of Iowa, Fall 2004.

85   *doing research on*: Harvey Mansfield as quoted in "America's Best Colleges," *U.S. News & World Report,* August 29, 2005.

88   *scholars do scholarship*: Stanley N. Katz, "Liberal Education on the Ropes," *Chronicle of Higher Education,* April 1, 2005.

89   *"helpfulness" and "availability"*: Samantha Stainburn, "The Case of the Vanishing Full-time Professor," Education Life, *New York Times,* December 30, 2009. A table with the figures laid out in this section accompanied Stainburn's original article. This table, unfortunately, is not available online.

90   *primary activities*: Unfortunately, the original position paper is no longer available from the university. For similar views on the

university's position, please see Armond Spencer, "On Attracting and Retaining Mathematics Majors," *Notices of the American Mathematical Society* (August 1995).

91 *is overwhelming*: David Harris as quoted in Laura Pappano, "How to Survive the Lecture Course," Education Life, *New York Times*, January 6, 2008.

92 *upward of half*: Task Force on Teaching and Career Development, *A Compact to Enhance Teaching and Learning at Harvard*, Harvard University, January 2007.

104 *Costco's chief executive*: "CEO Profiles," report by SpencerStuart, management consulting firm, 2005.

107 *the abilities necessary*: W. Norton Grubb and Marvin Lazerson, *The Education Gospel* (Harvard University Press, 2004).

116 *faster than inflation*: Jonathan D. Glater and Alan Finder, "In Tuition Price, Popularity Rises with Price," *New York Times*, December 12, 2006.

119 *a jumbo Jacuzzi*: Greg Winter, "Jacuzzi U.? A Battle of Perks to Lure Students," *New York Times*, October 5, 2003.

119 *Dijon chicken*: Michael S. Sanders, "Latest College Reading Lists: Menus with Pho and Lobster," *New York Times*, April 9, 2008.

120 *deficit of $3.6 billion*: Eric Dexheimer, "The Longhorn Economy," *Austin American-Statesman*, September 30, 2007.

121 *actually default and face foreclosures*: Norman Silber as quoted in Stephanie Strom, "Nonprofits Paying Price for Gamble in Finances," *New York Times*, September 23, 2009.

121 *told the lawmakers*: Shirley Tilghman, testifying before a joint-congressional hearing during an informal roundtable on September 8, 2008. The roundtable was conducted by Senator Charles Grassley and Representative Peter Welch. For more information, please see Tamar Lewin, "College Presidents Defend Rising Tuition, but Lawmakers Sound Skeptical," *New York Times*, September 8, 2008.

122 *most sued institutions*: Charles Huckabee, "U. of Iowa Paid $226,000 to Professor Accused of Forging Student Evaluations,"

Chronicle of Higher Education, April 8, 2007; Katharine Managan, "Former Medical Dean at U. of Florida Quits Faculty Post in $517,000 Settlement," *Chronicle of Higher Education*, July 20, 2009; Libby Sander, "U. of Colorado at Boulder Settles Lawsuit Over Alleged Rapes at Football Recruiting Party for $2.85 Million," *Chronicle of Higher Education*, December 6, 2007; "La Salle U. Will Pay $7.5-Million in Settlement Over Athlete's Concussion," The Ticker, *Chronicle of Higher Education*, December 1, 2009; Charles Huckabee, "Charleston Southern U. Will Pay $3.9-Million to Settle Charges Tied to Former Professor," *Chronicle of Higher Education*, February 5, 2008.

123　*inability to pay*: William G. Bowen, Martin A. Kurzweil, and Eugene M. Tobin, *Equity and Excellence in American Higher Education* (University of Virginia Press, 2005).

124　*pay for a car*: Gaston Caperton as quoted in Libby Sander, "Tuition Increases at Public Colleges Outpace Those at Private Institutions, Survey Finds," *Chronicle of Higher Education*, October 22, 2007.

125　*life had fallen apart*: *Student Loan Sinkhole,* Public Broadcasting System, June 18, 2009.

129　*after Pell grants*: "Trends in College Pricing," Trends in Higher Education Series, College Board, 2009. A PDF version is available at http://www.trends-collegeboard.com/college_pricing/pdf/2009_Trends_College_Pricing.pdf.

130　*conducts annual surveys*: Table 3: Age of Reference Person, Consumer Expenditures—2008, U.S. Bureau of Labor Statistics, U.S. Department of Labor, October 6, 2009. A PDF version is available at http://www.bls.gov/cex/2008/Standard/age.pdf.

130　*parents had put anything aside*: "Trends in Student Aid," Trends in Higher Education Series, College Board, 2009. A PDF version is available at http://www.trends-collegeboard.com/student_aid/pdf/2009_Trends_Student_Aid.pdf.

133　*uninhibited scholarship*: *AAUP v. Bloomfield College* 322 A.2d 846 (N.J. Super. Ct. 1974).

134 *philosophical key*: Louis Menand, *The Marketplace of Ideas* (W.W. Norton and Company, 2010).

134 *controversial professors*: James Garland, *Saving Alma Mater* (University of Chicago Press, 2009).

136 For details on these and other cases, see the Censure List of the American Association of University Professors (AAUP), available on their website, and the Cases & Issues section on the Foundation for Individual Rights in Education (FIRE) website.

138 *Dark Night field notes*: This essay was originally published on Churchill's personal website (http://ratical.com) under the title "Some People Push Back: On the Justice of Roosting Chickens," supplement of "Dark Nights field notes," *Pockets of Resistance*, no. 11 (September 12, 2001). It was later republished in his 2003 book, *On the Justice of Roosting Chickens* (AK Press).

140 *case to court*: *Churchill v. University of Colorado* 06CV11473 (Denver Dist. Ct. 2009).

141 *Faculty with tenure*: Lionel S. Lewis, *Cold War on Campus* (Transaction Publishers, 1987).

143 *sexuality became a weapon*: Harris Mirkin, "The Pattern of Sexual Politics: Feminism, Homosexuality and Pedophilia," *Journal of Homosexuality* 37, no. 2 (February 1999).

146 *free to write*: Louis Menand, ed., *The Future of Academic Freedom* (University of Chicago Press, 1996).

148 *an original idea*: Garland, *Saving Alma Mater.*

149 *equitable expectations*: Scott Jaschik, "Defeating Post-Tenure Review," *Inside Higher Ed*, March 25, 2009.

150 *fear of litigation*: J. Peter Byrne, *Academic Freedom without Tenure*, New Pathways Series (Stylus Publishing, 1997).

153 *Yeshiva decision*: *National Labor Relations Board v. Yeshiva University* 444 U.S. 672 (1980).

153 *Grain by grain*: Richard Chait, ed., *The Questions of Tenure* (Harvard University Press, 2002).

157 *won't try to echo*: Murray Sperber, *Beer and Circus* (Holt

Paperbacks, 2001); William Dowling, *Confessions of a Spoilsport* (Penn State Press, 2007).

159   *In return for pulling an oar*: Juliet Macur, "Never Rowed? Take a Free Ride," *New York Times,* May 28, 2004.

162   *water polo team*: Joshua Robinson, "Everybody Into the Talent Pool," *New York Times,* September 19, 2007.

163   *wrestling teams lost*: John Irving, "Wrestling With Title IX," *New York Times,* January 28, 2003.

167   *Day after day*: Estep Nagy, letter to the editor, *New York Review of Books,* September 20, 2001.

169   *require surgery in a typical year*: James J. Duderstadt, *Intercollegiate Athletics and the American University* (University of Michigan Press, 2000).

172   *research we've reviewed*: See especially Robert H. Frank, *Challenging the Myth: A Review of the Links Between College Athletic Success, Student Quality, and Donations* (Knight Foundation Commission, 2004).

173   *listed all gifts*: "Major Private Gifts to Higher Education Since 1967," *Chronicle of Higher Education,* August 24, 2009.

177   *contested affirmative action*: *Grutter v. Bollinger* 539 U.S. 306 (2003); *Gratz v. Bollinger* 539 U.S. 244 (2003).

180   *The best study*: James L. Shulman and William G. Bowen, *The Game of Life* (Princeton University Press, 2001).

180   *also parsed the records*: Thomas J. Espenshade, Chang Y. Chung, and Joan L. Walling, "Admission Preferences for Minority Students, Athletes, and Legacies at Elite Universities," *Social Science Quarterly*, December 2004; Thomas J. Espenshade and Chang Y. Chung, "The Opportunity Cost of Admission Preference at Elite Universities," *Social Science Quarterly*, June 2005.

182   *not Mary and Mary*: "A Reverse Gender Gap?" *Newsweek* supplementary issue "How to Get Into College," 2008.

184   *top economic quintile*: Ron Haskins, "Economic and Social Mobility," in Ron Haskins, Julia Isaacs, and Isabel Sawhill, eds. *Getting Ahead or Losing Ground* (Brookings Institution, 2008).

187 *42 most selective*: David Leonhardt, "As Wealthy Fill Top Colleges, Concerns Grow Over Fairness," *New York Times*, April 22, 2004.

195 *improve student learning*: Carol A. Twigg, "Improving Learning and Reducing Costs," *EDUCAUSE Review* 38, no. 5 (September/October 2003).

201 *Intelligent Essay Assessor*: A. James Wohlpart, Chuck Lindsey, and Craig Rademacher, "The Reliability of Computer Software to Score Essays," *Computers and Composition* 25, no. 2 (2008): 203–23.

205 *take some students*: Edward B. Fiske, "New Secretary Sees Many 'Ripped Off' in Higher Education," *New York Times*, February 12, 1985.

207 *office supply order*: Margaret Spellings, "A Test of Leadership: Charting the Future of United States Higher Education," The Secretary of Education's Commission on Higher Education, U.S. Department of Higher Education, 2006.

208 *more knowledgeable*: Ernest T. Pascarella and Patrick T. Terenzini, *How College Affects Students*, 2 vols. (Jossey-Bass, 1991 and 2005), 577, 581, 585.

211 *party registrations*: Daniel B. Klein and Charlotte Stern, "Professors and Their Politics," *American Sociologist* 17, nos. 3 and 4 (Summer 2005): 257–303.

211 *sentiments about abortion*: "Pragmatic Americans Liberal and Conservative on Social Issues," Pew Research Center, survey report, August 3, 2006.

216 *top-ranked schools*: Stacy Berg Dale and Alan B. Krueger, "Estimating the Payoff to Attending a More Selective College," *Quarterly Journal of Economics* 107, no. 4 (November 2002): 1491–1527.

238 *no parent should*: "Paying for School Special," Suze Orman website Resource Center, February 2010.

238 *their dissertation*: William Bennett as quoted in Malcolm Scully, "Concern of Professors Must Be Aroused if Reforms of College

Education Are to Take Place, Critics Say," *Chronicle of Higher Education*, February 20, 1985, page 19.

240 *rewards conformity*: Cristina Nehring, "Is Tenure a Matter of Life or Death?" *Chronicle of Higher Education*, February 21, 2010.

241 *Haverford and Davidson*: Richard Vedder, et. al, *Outcomes Based Assessment of Universities*, Center for College Affordability and Productivity, March 1, 2008.

ACKNOWLEDGMENTS

Claudia Dreifus would like to extend thanks to John Coatsworth, Dan McIntyre, Anya Schiffrin, Steven Cohen, Louise Rosen, Audrey Lapiner, and Lourdes Gautier for creating an exemplary teaching environment at Columbia University's School of International and Public Affairs. And also to her editors at the *New York Times*, Laura Chang, David Corcoran, and Jim Gorman. Andrew Hacker expresses similar appreciation to Patricia Rachal, Jim Muyskens, and Iris Braun at Queens College.

Parts of this book first appeared, in somewhat different forms, in the *New York Review of Books*, and we are grateful to them for permission to reprint this material. We owe particular thanks to Robert Silvers and the late Barbara Epstein for their incisive suggestions and continuing support.

When people heard of the subject we had chosen, many helpful conversations ensued. We learned a lot from Larry Arbeiter, Helen Barron, Eleanor Baum, Ernst Benjamin, Robert Berdahl, Robert Berman, George Black, Julian Bond, Anne-Marie Bouche, George Campbell Jr., Sean Carroll, Julia Cass, Rebecca Chopp, Janina

Ciezadlo, Matt Clemons, Lizabeth Cohen, Steven Cohen, Donald Cole, Rita Colwell, Blanche Weisen Cook, Stephanie Coontz, Clare Coss, Michael Crow, Laura Couglan, Tracy Day, Cornelia Dean, James Diorio, Ron Dorfman, Troy Duster, Cynthia Fuchs Epstein, Edward Jay Epstein, Paul Fain, Hany Farid, Jaime Farrare, Dan Friedland, William Friedland, Ester Fuchs, Eva Gadja, Tom Glaisyer, Rainer Glaser, Bill Goldstein, Ann Gower, Timothy Gower, Victoria Gray, Brian Greene, Vartan Gregorian, Susannah Heschel, Catherine Hill, Marvine Howe, Freeman Hrabowski, Ken Illio, Harvey Jay, Jerome Karabel, Stanley Katz, Nan Keohane, Randall Kennedy, Robert C. Khayat, Chuck Kleinhans, Jill Kozney, Kitty Krupat, Carolyn LeGuin, Charles LeGuin, Ursula LeGuin, Julia Lesage, Mike Levitas, Lionel Lewis, William Lipkin, Mitchell Lipton, Jane Lubchenko, Alison Lurie, Jeff Madrick, John Maeda, Kate Maloff, Anthony Marx, Avice Meehan, Bruce Menge, Dennis Meredith, John Merrow, Maryisa Navarro Aranguren, Anne Nelson, Catherine Theimer Nepomnyashchy, Hana Newman, Carolyn Toll Oppenheim, Tom Parker, Paul Przyblowicz, Shaun Randol, Ward Regan, Kevin Reilly, Virgil Renzulli, Sam Roberts, Daniel Rose, Don Rose, Joanna Rose, Andrew Ross, Michael Sandel, Bernice Sandler, Chris Sargent, Pepper Schwartz, Joel Schlemowitz, Cynthia Scaggs Scurria, Desiree Segura, Barbara Seidman, Joan Milkin Silver, Ray Silver, Barbara Probst Solomon, Debora Spar, Robert Squillace, Michael Summers, Analyn Swan, Albert Teich, Samantha Teich, Gloria Thomas, Cindy Lee Van Dover, Isiah Warner, Carl Wieman, Jim Wohlpart, Robert Wilkes, Don Wycliff, and Curtis Yehnert.

Robin Straus, our agent and friend for many years, has always been on hand with professional counsel and personal understanding. *Higher Education?* owes more than we can say to the commitment of our Holt editors, production editor, and designer. Paul Golob, Robin Dennis, Emi Ikkanda, Dedi Felman, Kathleen Cook, and Kelly Too provided every kind of help and encouragement authors want and need.

We want to include the American Association of University Professors and *The Chronicle of Higher Education* on this page because they are much more than editorial sources; they are genuine national institutions. Any understanding of the academic world has to build on the information they gather and the data they collate.

INDEX

ABOUT THE AUTHORS

ANDREW HACKER is the author of the bestselling *Two Nations: Black & White, Separate, Hostile, Unequal* and writes regularly for the *New York Review of Books* and other publications. He is a professor at Queens College.

CLAUDIA DREIFUS is a writer for the "Science Times" section of the *New York Times* and an adjunct associate professor at Columbia University's School of International and Public Affairs.

They live in New York City.

For more information about the authors, go to highereducationquestionmark.com.